Applications

of

Modern

High Performance

Networks

Wireless Sensor Networks, Ultra Wide Band, Mobile Ad-Hoc Networks, Computer Clusters, Smart Agriculture and Distance Computing

Junaid Ahmed Zubairi

Editor

State University of New York at Fredonia

TABLE OF CONTENTS

FOREWORD

In my academic and research career spanning over 15 years, I have hardly met people who are as dedicated and hardworking to research and its dissemination as the editors of this ebook. Time and again they have sacrificed their time and resources to share fundamental research contributions with a broader audience in the form of tutorials, workshops, and hands-on free labs on topics related to networking and applications.

This time around they have put together a highly balanced edited volume consisting of computer networking applications ranging from basic networking technologies, to diverse applications such as agriculture and distance computing, covering a broad spectrum of applications. It introduces the readers to basic networking technologies and then takes them to its use in modern day applications. For example, the chapters dealing with computer clusters contain practical hands-on guides to building and deploying Linux based Beowulf and SSI (Single System Image) clusters. This ebook is an interesting and stimulating collection of chapters and a must read for graduate students, practitioners, and researchers interested in networking applications.

Ashfaq A. Khokhar,

Ph.D. , IEEE Fellow

Professor, Department of Electrical and Computer Engineering

University of Illinois at Chicago, USA.

PREFACE

The history of networks and communications goes back to the age when smoke was used to transmit and receive information between two entities. Today, networking has reached the stage where it finds its far reaching applications in numerous fields of everyday life. This book takes a look at some of these applications of modern high performance networks. Modern networks are rapidly becoming ubiquitous and reliable. With the integration of wireless and wired networks and with the increase in the available bandwidth, newer applications are being deployed that were not imagined a few years ago. For example, transparent international roaming of voice line subscribers, use of networks to transmit emergency medical data to hospitals, delivery of important information to farmers about weather and impending harms for crops and control and monitoring of municipal utilities via browser interface. These and other new applications have only become possible after a number of new developments including the proliferation of network enabled devices such as cellular phones and personal digital assistants on a massive scale. The other important developments include the enabling of multi Gigabit optical fibre core network and the development of QoS protocols for the wired and wireless networks.

There has been little effort in bringing together diverse applications of networks under one title. This book is aimed at academicians, students and working professionals in Hospitals, Agriculture, Government, Military, and Networking technology fields. The book has been compiled focusing on the state-of-the-art research and development in modern high performance networks. Hence, I hope that it will provide a useful guideline and resource to researchers working in these areas or intending to embark upon one or more of these areas. It is also intended for readers to understand how the networks are affecting our lives.

The topics covered in this book include the following:

- ∞ Mobile ad-hoc networks
- ∞ Clusters for distance computing
- ∞ Clustering technologies and deployment
- ∞ Emerging Wireless sensor network technologies
- ∞ Ultra Wideband Wireless Sensor networks
- ∞ Smart agriculture with sensor networks

Each chapter has an abstract and keywords followed by introduction and other sections. Readers can determine their interest level in the chapter quickly by using the keywords and abstract. The chapters on clustering include practical steps in deploying a cluster some of which are tried and tested methods and others are experiments as conducted by author(s). The chapters on sensor networks expand from the basic sensor network technology to the emerging branches such as WMSN, WSAN and UWB based sensor networks.

I thank my co-editor Dr. Imran Tasadduq for providing useful support during the editing process. I would also like to thank the reviewers who took the time to go over the submitted chapters and provided useful feedback that improved the overall quality of the book.. I appreciate and thank my wife Shagufta for being supportive of this project and for being patient while I worked on this project.

Junaid Ahmed Zubairi
Ph.D.
State University of New York, Fredonia, NY, USA.

LIST OF CONTRIBUTING AUTHORS

Shakeel Durrani
National University of Sciences & Technology, Pakistan. shakeel.durrani@gmail.com

Nassar Ikram
National University of Sciences & Technology, Pakistan. dr_nassar_ikram@yahoo.com;

K. S. Kwak
UWB Wireless Communications Research Center, Inha University, Korea

Athar Mahboob
National University of Sciences & Technology, Pakistan. atharmahboob@yahoo.com

S. Mehta
UWB Wireless Communications Research Center, Inha University, Korea. suryanand.m@gmail.com

Syed Misbahuddin
Department of Computer Science and Software Engineering, University of Hail, Saudi Arabia.
doctorsyedmisbah@yahoo.com

Fazal Noor
Department of Computer Science and Software Engineering, University of Hail, Saudi Arabia.
fnoor@uoh.edu.sa

Mahmood Qureshi
Department of Electrical Engg ,COMSATS Institute of Information Technology , Islamabad, Pakistan.
mehmoodqureshi@comsats.edu.pk;

Aqeel-ur-Rehman
Dept. of Computer Science, National University of Computer and Emerging Sciences (FAST-NU),
Pakistan. aqeel.rehman@nu.edu.pk;

Husnain Saeed
National University of Sciences & Technology, Pakistan. husnain.saeed@gmail.com

Hasan Sajid
National University of Sciences & Technology, Pakistan. hasan.sajid@gmail.com

Zubair A. Shaikh
Dept. of Computer Science, National University of Computer and Emerging Sciences (FAST-NU),
Pakistan. zubairi@fredonia.edu

Junaid A. Zubairi
Department of Computer Science, State University of New York at Fredonia, USA.
Junaid.Zubairi@fredonia.edu

About the Editor

Junaid Ahmed Zubairi , Ph.D. is an Associate Professor in the Department of Computer and Information Sciences at State University of New York at Fredonia. Dr. Zubairi received his BE (Electrical Engineering) from NED University of Engineering, Pakistan and MS and Ph.D. (Computer Engineering) from Syracuse University, USA. He worked in Sir Syed University Pakistan and Intl' Islamic University Malaysia before joining SUNY at Fredonia in 1999. Dr. Zubairi is a recipient of many awards including Pakistan Government Science and Technology scholarship for postgraduate studies, Malaysian Government IRPA (Intensification of Research in Priority Areas) research award, National Science Foundation MACS (Math and Computer Science) award, SUNY Scholarly Incentive award and SUNY Faculty Fellowship award. He has published several book chapters, journal articles and conference papers in his areas of interest. His research interests include network applications, traffic engineering and performance evaluation of networks. He can be reached at junaid.zubairi@fredonia.edu

CHAPTER 1

Single Path and Multi-Path Routing Survey for Mobile Ad-Hoc Networks

Mahmood Qureshi*

Department of Electrical Engineering, COMSATS Institute of Information Technology , Islamabad, Pakistan.

Abstract: Mobile Ad Hoc Network (MANET) is a multi-hop wireless link, without any infrastructure and frequent host mobility. MANET Routing Protocols play a vital role to transfer data from one mobile node to another. There are variety of routing MANET algorithms exists but it is difficult to decide which protocol is more suitable for the particular environment. In this paper we investigate different kinds of MANETs single path and multipath routing protocols and compare the performance by considering the factors like bandwidth, throughput, packets delivery ratio, power consumption etc. which helps to analyze the performance of the network. These protocols are listed under certain category.

INTRODUCTION

The quantity and variety of wireless devices and applications has dramatically increased within the past few years. In an effort to establish and maintain routing paths in these ad hoc mobile networks [1] also called MANET (Mobile Ad hoc Network), numerous single path and multi path protocols have been designed. MANET is wireless network having no infrastructure. There is no need to pre-install the base stations in MANET. Each node in these networks act as a router, and data packets can be transmit and received through these nodes. Ad hoc networks can be used for communication in ad hoc settings such as in conferences or classrooms [2].

MANETs include easy installation and upgrade, because there is no need to install the new hardware like routers, hubs, switches and other basics components of the networks. MANET provides more flexibility and the ability to employ new and efficient routing protocols for wireless communication. As nodes mobility and network size increase, the performance degrades and the control overhead and computational complexity increases non-linearly [3]. Node mobility also effect the performance in MANET causing the link in route may become temporarily unavailable and making the route invalid. The alternative routes may cause extra delay in packet delivery. To overcome such kinds of problem multi path is used in MANET.

A major problem in MANET is to deliver data packets to other node efficiently. As MANET usually have limited memory so it is difficult to store the whole topology especially in the large networks hence routing in such networks is tough and challenging task. A lot of routing algorithms have been proposed for Ad hoc networks and some of them have been widely used.

In this chapter different flavor of MANET routing protocols has been explored. All the listed protocols fall under two categories which are single path routing protocol, and multipath scheme. Efforts have been put to address the most important questions in Ad hoc networking routing protocols which can benefit for the small and high density networks. We also discuss the characteristics which increase the performance of the networks and the factors that take part to degrade the performance of MANET.

We present protocols that solve the listed limitations problems.

- Packets loss due to transmission errors

- Frequent disconnections/partitions
- Limited communication bandwidth
- Broadcast nature of the communication
- Short batteries
- Limited capacity

SINGLE PATH AND MULTI-PATH ROUTING

Single Path is the oldest method of routing. In single path or uni-path routing, the source node can send the packet from source node to destination node by following the only single path, router usually select the best route to each destination. The other advantage we can achieve is less traffic congested and easily implementable. But also degrade the performance of MANET like consuming more energy and less throughputs.

Multipath routing allows two or more than two network nodes to exchange messages over multiple paths [4]. It is not a new concept in routing, in data network the idea of using multiple paths for end-to-end transport first appeared in 1975 [5]. Traditional circuit switched telephone networks used a type of multipath routing called alternate path routing. The main purpose of using multi-path routing is to perform better load balancing and to grant high fault tolerance [4].

When link is broken on a path there is no need to route discovery process again. Which increase the overall performance in the factor like end-to-end delay, throughput and fault tolerance.

The use of multiple paths between a source and destination can facilitate load balancing, higher aggregate bandwidth, increase data throughput [6], reduced traffic congestion[7], Improved network utilization[8], [9], and enhanced data security [10], [11], [12] and improve robustness [13], [14], [15].

ROUTING PROTOCOL

Mobile Ad hoc network became a hot topic for research especially for notebook and other handheld mobile devices like PDA (Personal Digital Assistant), cell phone etc in the mid to late 1990s. Up till now many researchers contributed their efforts in the MANET by proposing their own protocols. Hundreds of protocols have been proposed for MANET but it is difficult to decide which protocol will provide the better result under some specific condition, there is no single protocol which that works well in scenarios with different network nodes, node mobility pattern and traffic overloads. To overcome this problem we classify the major protocols under some category which are listed below.

Proactive routing calculates routes before they are really needed. It is a simple naïve approach to keep up-to-date all nodes periodically. Contrary to this, Reactive routing comes in action to calculate route on event-driven bases. It needs not to propagate routing information periodically, thereby reducing network overhead.

Hybrid routing is packaged with both proactive and reactive routing flavors. The rationale behind hybrid routing is that routes are initially maintained proactively but later can adopt reactive routing approach as per demand. Hierarchical routing is a projection of Hybrid routing from flat to multi-layer MANET.

Geographical routing optimizes route calculation mechanism by implying the significance of spatial location with respect to network performance. Usually they use Global Position System (GPS) for routing. When it comes to make best use of available energy for limited resource MANET, power-aware routing is the best option. Security-aware routing arranges a security path for routing with respect to the security level specified by mobile node.

Multicasting routing deals with the mechanism of packet transmission to ad hoc groups of mobile nodes in order to optimize energy and bandwidth. In order to mitigate the concern for link break during mobility, different network characteristics are measured or predicted to ensure link availability during transmission of packets.

Adaptive routing is another version of hybrid routing where the difference lies when it comes to read the situation on ad hoc basis. Channel-aware routing maintains multiple routes that use different channels so that in case of absence of running channel, other channel can be utilized to ensure transmission.

- Proactive Routing (Table-Driven)
- Reactive Routing (On-Demand)
- Hybrid Routing (blend of Reactive and Proactive)
- Hierarchical (Zone/Cluster-Based) Routing Protocols
- Geographical Routing Protocols (Location based)
- Power-Aware Routing Protocols
- Multicasting Routing Protocols
- Adaptive Routing (Situation Aware)

All the above mentioned protocols are categorized according to different design philosophies and proposed to meet specific requirement from different application domain.

PROACTIVE ROUTING PROTOCOL

Proactive routing protocols maintain routes updates to all destinations all the time, by periodically distributing routing tables throughout the network, regardless of whether or not these routes are needed. Proactive Protocols check the table to find the route to the destination that is why they are also known as Table Driven Protocols. Most Famous Protocols for single path are Destination Sequenced Distance Vector (DSDV)[16], Wireless Routing Protocol (WRP)[17] while Multipath Destination Sequenced Distance Vector (MDSDV) [18] and Tree Exchange Routing Algorithm (TERA) [19] are Multi-path protocols. The main advantage and disadvantage of Proactive Routing Protocols are

Pros:

- Minimal initial delay.
- Quickly establish a session.
-     Hosts can quickly obtain route information.

Cons:

- High storage requirement.

- Periodic update is required in proactive.
- Slow reaction on restructuring and failures.
- Bandwidth wastage is observed because of unnecessarily control messages are sent out even when there is no data traffic.

Single Path

1) DSDV:

DSDV is table-driven routing algorithm. DSDV is MANET based on the Bellman-Ford algorithm [20]. Sequence numbers is used to prevent the loop problem. Routing information is distributed between nodes via periodically updates. "Settling time" metric is used to determine update interval. DSDV have considerable difficulties in maintaining valid routes, and loses many packets because of that behavior [21].

Pros:

- Simple to implement
- Avoid the Route Loop problem.
- No latency caused by routing discovery
- Suitable for small networks

Cons:

- Requires a regular update of its routing tables by sending lots of control message
- High Traffic Congestion
- High Power consumption and bandwidth wastage.
- New Sequence Number is required whenever the topology change
- Not suitable for highly dynamic networks so scalability is the disadvantage.
- Packets Delay increase with mobility.[21]
- Throughput is decreased when mobility is increased.
- Highest byte overhead because the routing table updates often contain the entire routing table.
- Large number of packets dropped due to invalid route.
- Large amount of memory is required.

2) WRP

Wireless Routing Protocol (WRP) uses improved Bellman-Ford Distance Vector routing algorithm [22]. Each mobile node maintains a distance table, a routing table, a link-cost table and a Message Retransmission List (MRL). The MRL contains information about which neighbor has not acknowledged an update message. By using update messages mobile nodes exchange routing tables with their neighbors. The update messages can be sent either periodically or whenever link state changes happen.

Pros:

- Node checks the consistency of its neighbors after detecting any link change, which helps to eliminate loops and speed up convergence.
- Avoids the count to infinity problem [23].
- Faster route convergence when a link failure event occur [24].

Cons:

- Limited Scalability.
- Not suitable for large MANET.
- Four tables Requires a large amount of memory.
- Periodic hello message consumes more power.
- Wastage of bandwidth because of periodic messages.
- Required high Computing Resource to Maintain Several Tables.

Multi-Path

3) MDSDV:

Multipath Destination Sequenced Distance Vector (MDSDV) guarantees loop freedom and disjointness of alternative paths. MDSDV finds disjoint paths which do not have any common nodes between a source and destination.[18] Two new fields called second hop and link-id are used to construct these disjoint paths. Both second hop and link-id which is generated by the destination are used to get disjoint paths from any source to any destination. MDSDV employs a unique method of creating routing tables containing the optimal paths to every destination. Each node maintains two tables which are Routing Table (RT) and Neighbors Table (NT). RT lists a number of paths to each destination of the network. It maintains an up-to-date view of the network,

NT maintains a table which contains all its neighbors. By using this table, any node can determine its status. If this table is empty, the node considers itself as an isolated node which means that it has to propagate a hello message. NT is updated in case of receiving a hello message or when one of its neighbors goes out of its transmission range.

Pros:

- Faster and efficient recovery from Route Failure.
- Avoid route loop problem.

Cons:

- More bandwidth wastage
- Not suitable for highly dynamic networks.
- More Traffic congested then DSDV because number of control messages also increased.
- More Power consumption because now multiple nodes are participating to send the message.
- Increasing the mobility will decrease the effect of throughput.
- Highest byte overhead because the routing table updates often contain the entire routing table.

4) TERA

The basic idea of Tree Exchange Routing Algorithm (TERA) [25] is to split up a path between a source and a target node into two paths at every forwarding node resulting in multiple paths between source and target. TERA is based on asynchronous distributed distance vector routing but uses several additional tables to allow path reconstruction. Offers multipath routing based on the already available topology information, which does not require any additional routing messages to be sent at all. Just one additional step must be added to the processing of routing update messages to obtain an alternative packet forwarding possibility at each node. Whenever multiple paths are available, the forwarded data packets are later randomly distributed to each available path.

Pros:

- Avoids count to infinity problem[25]
- Bottleneck avoidance [19].
- Load distribution.
- Multiple-path can be set up at almost no additional cost.

Cons:

- Respective amount of data for maintenance
- A route breakdown of one path will result in loosing only the number of packets which has been sent to the broken path. So Increased Packets Loss [19].

REACTIVE ROUTING PROTOCOL

Reactive routing protocol finds a route on demand by flooding the network with Route Request packets. This protocol need not to maintain the routes so reduce routing overhead is observed. This property is very appealing in the resource-limited environment. Three different kinds of messages are circulating among the network [26] i.e. route request (RREQ) to request a new route when one node want to send data, route reply (RREP) after the successful discovery of destination node then the route reply message is forward back to the source node and route error (RERR) is use when an error occurred in the network like link broken etc.

Most famous protocols for Single path are Dynamic Source Routing (DSR) [26][27] and Ad hoc On Demand Distance Vector (AODV) [28] while Multipath Source Routing (MSR) [29] and Ad hoc On Demand Multipath Distance Vector (AOMDV) [30] are Multi-path protocols. The main advantage and disadvantage of Proactive Routing Protocols are

Pros:

- Memory efficient.
- Improve scalability.
- Reduce the control traffic overhead
- Hosts can quickly obtain route information
- Less Power consumption as compare to proactive protocols.
- Increase Reliability that is almost guaranteed to reach the destination.

Cons:

- Delay Occur before every Session.
- High Latency time in route finding.
- Excessive flooding can lead to network clogging.
- Bandwidth wastage because of flooding.

Single Path

5) DSR:

All nodes are willing to forward the packets to other nodes. In Dynamic Source Routing [26] [27] (DSR) protocol every data packet carries the whole path information in its header.

Pros:

- Does not require symmetric links.
- Intermediate nodes need not to keep routing information because path is explicitly specified in the data packets.
- Route caching reduce the cost of route discovery.
- A single route discovery may yield many routes to the destination, due to intermediate nodes may reply route request from local caches.

Cons:

- With time passing and node moving, cached routes may become invalid.
- Inefficiency; Packet header size grows with route length due to source routing.
- RREQ flooding.
- Route requests may collide at the targeted node
- No energy saving; every node needs to turn on its receiver all the time.
- Route Reply Storm; Increased contention if too many route replies come back
- Mess up routing and forwarding; an intermediate node may send Route Reply using a stale cached route, thus polluting other nodes' caches.
- Degrades rapidly with increasing mobility.

6) AODV

Ad hoc On-demand Distance Vector (AODV) builds on the DSDV Algorithm [31]. AODV follow the sequence numbering procedure of DSDV and for route discovery procedure it follows DSR Algorithm. It requests only a route when needed and does not require nodes to maintain routes to destinations that are not communicating [21] so it maintains the routing information only for the active path.

Pros:

- AODV is the efficient algorithm in the Ad hoc Network
- Adaptable to highly dynamic networks.
- Quick response in link breakage in active routes.
- Loop free routes by using sequence number.
- AODV save bandwidth for large MANET in sense of data packets do not carry the whole path information.

Cons:

- Large Delay during route construction and link failure.
- Periodic beaconing leads to unnecessary bandwidth consumption [32].
- There may be multiple RREP packets in response to a single RREQ.

Multi-Path

7) MSR:

Multipath Source Routing (MSR) is the extension of DSR. Although DSR can find multiple paths in the Route Discovery, it only uses the shortest path as routing criterion, so it is essentially a single path protocol. To overcome the disadvantage of single path routing on underutilizing resources and leading to congestion, MSR [29] sends packets over multiple paths collected in Route Discovery phase. In routes selection, the disjoint paths are preferred in MSR because a more independent path can provide more resources between two nodes. Delay is used as the metric to distribute packets over multiple routes and a periodic probing mechanism is deployed to obtain the dynamic delay information for each path in use. By load balancing, MSR not only improves the network utilization but also balances the energy consumption for each node so as to increase the network lifetime.

Pros:

- Improves the packet delivery ratio [29].
- Improve throughput
- Reduce the End to end delay
- Decrease the Network congestion.
- Load Distributed Scheme.
- Load balancing bye network utilization and energy consumption.

Cons:

- Processing Overhead.
- More Route Request Flooding
- Farther is the destination node heavier is the packet header.
- More Energy Consumption, because more mobile nodes are participating to send the packets from source node to destination node.
- More complex to implement.
- Require more routing table space.
- Computational overhead.

8) AOMDV:

Ad hoc On demand Multi-path Distance Vector routing (AOMDV) [30] is an extension to the AODV protocol for computing multiple loop-free and link-disjoint paths. The general concept is shown in the Section III. Beside that given figure 7 showing the procedure.

In the intermediate nodes, unlike in AODV, duplicate copies of RREQ are not immediately discarded. Each copy is examined to see if it provides a new node disjoint path to the source. This is ascertained by examining the firsthop field in the RREQ copy and the firsthop_list in the node for the RREQ. If it does provide a new path, the AOMDV route update rule is invoked to check if a reverse path can be setup. If a reverse path is set up and a valid route to the destination is available at the intermediate node it sends back a RREP to the source. Just as in AODV, only the first arriving RREQ copy is forwarded if a route to destination is unavailable.

At the destination, reverse routes are setup just like in the case of intermediate nodes. However, in the hope of getting link-disjoint paths, the destination node adopts a "looser" reply policy. It replies upto k copies of RREQ arriving via unique neighbors. Unique neighbors guarantee link disjointness in the first hop of the RREP.

Pros:

- AOMDV allows intermediate nodes to reply to RREQs, while still selecting disjoint paths.
- Lower Latency.
- Better Performance in route discovery.

Cons:

- More messages overhead during route discovery because of increased flooding.
- Destinations replies to multiple RREQs, causing longer overhead.
- Complexity overhead as compare to single path.
- Can result in packets reordering.
- Maintaining multiple routes to the destination results in larger routing table at intermediate node.

HYBRID ROUTING PROTOCOL

Hybrid routing protocol possess both the properties of proactive routing as well as reactive routing. Mostly they are in the hierarchical form. There is low overhead of control messages in reactive protocol and low latency in proactive protocol. Hybrid protocols exploit the good features of both protocols. In hybrid protocol, routing is initially established by proactive routing and then serves the demand by the help of reactive protocol using flooding scheme. Typical example which lies under hybrid protocol for single path is Zone Routing Protocol (ZRP) [33], while Ant Agents for Hybrid Multipath Routing in Mobile Ad Hoc Networks (AntHocNet) [34] is the famous example for multi path hybrid network. The main pros and cons are listed below:

Pros:

- Advantage depends on amount of nodes activated.
- Reaction to traffic demand depends on gradient of traffic volume.
- Less Traffic Congested, less routing traffic than a pure reactive / proactive scheme.

Cons:

- Required More Memory.
- Scalability [32]

Single Path

9) ZRP:

Zone Routing Protocol (ZRP) in that case the network is partitioned or seen as a number of zones by each node. ZRP is formed by two sub-protocols, Intra-zone Routing Protocol (IARP) under the umbrella of proactive routing, where as Inter-zone Routing Protocol (IERP) is used inside routing zones and a following the reactive routing protocol.

Pros:

- Reduced Delay even less then DSR[32].

- Reduces the wastage of bandwidth and control overhead compared to reactive schemes
- Reduced the amount of communication overhead [32].

Cons:

- The large overlapping of routing zone.
- More storage is required for large networks.
- For large values of routing zone the protocol can behave like a pure proactive protocol, while for small values it behaves like a reactive protocol.

Multi-Path

10) AntHocNet:

Ant Agents for Hybrid Multipath Routing in Mobile Ad Hoc Networks (AntHocNet) is hybrid protocol for multipath. The main idea is based on Nature inspired Ant Colony Optimization (ACO) framework [34]. The main catalyst of this colony-level path behavior is the use of a volatile chemical substance called pheromone: ants moving between the nest and a food source deposit pheromone, and preferentially move in the direction of areas of higher pheromone intensity.

The network periodically and asynchronously sends out artificial ants towards possible destination nodes of data. These ants are small control packets, which have the task to find a path towards their destination and gather information about it. After the route setup, data packets are routed stochastically over the different paths following these pheromone tables. While the data session is going on, the paths are monitored, maintained and improved proactively using different agents, called proactive forward ants. The algorithm reacts to link failures with either a local route repair or by warning preceding nodes on the paths.

The route setup of this scheme is performed by reactive algorithm and the route probing and exploration are done by proactive scheme.

Pros:

- AntHocNet can outperform AODV in terms of delivery ratio and average delay, especially in more mobile and larger [34].
- Higher Delivery ratio
- Control overhead per packet is reduces
- Scalability.
- Connectivity.
- Reliability.
- Load Balancing

Cons:

- More Power consumption.
- Packets disordering can occur.
- Delay in route discovery.
- Very complex to implement.

HIERARCHICAL ROUTING PROTOCOLS

Hierarchical routing protocols often group routers together by function into a hierarchy [35]. Its Algorithm is based on link state [36]. The routing is initially established with some proactively prospected routes and then serves the demand from additionally activated nodes through reactive flooding on the lower levels

These types or protocols are difficult to implement because of complexity. This protocol also requires proper attribution for respective levels.

Hierarchical State Routing (HSR) [38] is the example of hierarchical routing used for single path. Cluster Based Routing Protocol (CBRP) [39] where as Hierarchical Max-Flow Routing (HMFR) [40] lie under the multipath category of Hierarchical Routing Protocol. The main advantage and disadvantage of Proactive Routing Protocols are

Pros:

- Best suitable for large networks.
- Drastic reduction of routing table storage.
- Avoid excessive overhead by limiting the local traffic to the local management.
- Only the global movements are reported between zones/hierarchical layers.
- Increased data throughput.

Cons:

- Increase the complexity of the routing scheme [41].
- Advantage depends on depth of nesting and addressing scheme.
- Reaction to traffic demand depends on meshing parameters.
- Delay is increased as well as the network size is increased.
- Mobility and Location management.

Single Path

11) HSR:

Hierarchical State Routing (HSR) follow the concept of multi-level clusters based hierarchical routing protocol i.e. mobile nodes are group into clusters and clusterhead is elected for each cluster. The clusterheads of low level clusters again organize themselves into upper level clusters, and so on. Inside a cluster, nodes broadcast their link state information to all others. Nodes in upper level hierarchical clusters flood the network topology information they have obtained to the nodes in the lower level clusters. The clusterhead summarizes link state information of its cluster and sends the information to its neighboring clusterheads via gateway nodes [38]. Gateways nodes can communicate with multiple cluster heads and thus can be reached from the top hierarchy via multiple paths. Consequently, a gateway has multiple hierarchical addresses, similar to a router in the wired Internet, equipped with multiple subnet addresses.

In HSR, hierarchical addressing is used and the network may have a recursive multi-level cluster structure. Moreover, a location management mechanism is used in HSR to map the logical address to the physical address.

Pros:

- Because of Hierarchy Routing Table size is reduced.

Cons:

- More Traffic Congestion. The process of exchanging information concerned all the levels of the hierarchy.
- Introduces extra overheads to the network from cluster formation and maintenance.

12) CBRP

Cluster Based Routing Protocol (CBRP) is grouped into clusters. Cluster-head is responsible for coordinating the data transmission within the cluster and to other clusters. The cluster members send the data to the cluster head (CH) and CH routes the data to the destination.

In CBRP, every node maintains a neighbor table in which it stores the information about link states (uni-directional or bi-directional) and the state of its neighbors. In addition to the information of all members in its cluster, a clusterhead keeps information of its neighboring clusters, which includes the clusterheads of neighboring clusters and gateway nodes connecting it to neighboring clusters.

If a source node wants to send a packet but has no active route which can be used, it floods route request to clusterhead of its own and all neighboring clusters. If a clusterhead receives a request it has seen before, it discards the request. Otherwise, the clusterhead checks if the destination of the request is in its cluster. If the destination is in the same cluster, the clusterhead sends the request to the destination, or it floods the request to its neighboring clusterheads. Source routing is used during the route search procedure and only the addresses of clusterheads on the route are recorded. The destination sends a reply including the route information recorded in the request if it successfully receives a route request. If the source doesn't receive a reply in the specified time period, it starts an exponentially backoff algorithm and sends the request later.

In CBRP, every node keeps information about its neighbors and a clusterhead maintains information about its members and its neighboring clusterheads. CBRP exploits the source routing scheme and the addresses of clusterheads along a route are recorded in the data packets.

Pros:

- Less control overhead because only the cluster heads exchange the information.
- Less flooding traffic during route discovery process.
- Broken route could be repaired locally without rediscovery.

Cons:

- The cluster head(s) is the one who dies very soon since its battery runs out quickly in comparison with the other nodes inside the cluster.
- Congestion at the cluster head is very high.
- Long Propagation Delay.
- More complicated route discovery is used.
- The protocol suffers from temporary routing loops. Because some nodes may carry inconsistent topology information due to long propagation delay.

- Not suitable for highly mobile environment because lots of HELLO messages are sent to maintain the cluster.

Multi-Path

13) HMFR:

Hierarchical Max-Flow Routing (HMFR) are very beneficial to avoid excessive overhead by limiting the local traffic to the local management and only global movements are observed between hierarchical/zone layers. But it also increases the complexity of the routing schemes. In [41] a technique (HMFR) is proposed to reduce the computational complexity of max-flow routing, based on a hierarchical decomposition of the network.

Pros:

- Forwards packets to minimize the impact of failures.
- Avoid excessive overhead.
- Less Congested Traffic.
- Best suitable for large networks.
- Increased the data throughput.
- Scalability is acting as the advantage factor.

Cons:

- May not provide the same level of robustness as flat routing.
- Large Memory Required.
- Computational complexity is quite high, making it not reasonable for moderate size networks.

GEOGRAPHICAL ROUTING PROTOCOLS

Geographic routing is also known as georouting or position-based routing. Geographic Routing Protocols relies on geographic position information. The main idea is to send the message from source to destination based on geographic location instead of network address. The source node is aware of the location of the destination. So there is no need to discover route and any additional knowledge of network topology.

Most of the single path routing protocols rely on two algorithms; greedy forwarding [42] and face routing [43]. Greedy forwarding helps to bring the message closer to the destination based on local information. Thus, each node forwards the message to the neighbor that is most suitable from a local point of view. The most suitable neighbor can be the one who minimizes the distance to the destination in each step (Greedy). Greedy forwarding can lead into a dead end, where there is no neighbor closer to the destination. Then facing routing helps to recover from that situation and find a path to another node, where greedy forwarding can be resumed. There are several protocols exist under geographic routing protocols. Most famous are Location Aided Routing Protocol (LAR) [44], Distance Routing Effect Algorithm for Mobility (DREAM) [45] , Geographic Location Service (GLS) [46], Connectivity-Aware Routing (CAR) [47] whereas Multipath Location Aided Routing Protocol (MLAR) [48] and Directional Antenna Multipath Location Aided Routing with On Demand Transmission Power (DA-MLAR-ODTP) [49] are lie under the multipath category.

Pros:

- Location Awareness.
- Minimum flooding.
- Bandwidth saving.
- Small memory is required.
- No latency caused by routing discovery

Cons:

- Efficiency depends on balancing the geographic distribution versus occurrence of traffic.
- Any dependence of performance with traffic load thwarting the negligence of distance may occur in overload.
- Loop free problem exist. (loop-free help to avoid timeout or memorizing past traffic)

Single Path

14) LAR:

Location Aided Routing Protocol (LAR) is reactive uni-cast on-demand routing protocol. In LAR, a source node estimates the current location range of the destination based on information of the last reported location and mobility pattern of the destination. In LAR, an expected zone is defined as a region that is expected to hold the current location of the destination node. During route discovery procedure, the route request flooding is limited to a request zone, which contains the expected zone and location of the sender node. Routing is done by last known location plus an assumption. In LAR the routing discovery is initiated when either the source node does not know the route to destination node or the previous route is broken.

Pros:

- Less congested traffic
- Decrease overhead of route discovery.
- Location awareness.
- Better performance in terms of routing discovery latency.

Cons:

- Not loop free.
- Scalability is the disadvantage.
- Each node is required to carry a GPS.
- Protocol may (for first method) behave similar to flooding protocol and in highly mobile networks

15) DREAM

In Distance Routing Effect Algorithm for Mobility (DREAM) based on proactive protocol, each node knows its geographical coordinates through a GPS [45]. These coordinates are periodically exchanged between each node and stored in a routing table (called a location table). When a source wants to send a packet, firstly it checks its routing table and gets the respective location information of the destination. Then, the source forwards the packet to a neighbor in the direction towards the destination. In DREAM, routing overhead is further reduced, by making the frequency at which update messages are disseminated proportional to mobility and the distance effect. Thus, stationary nodes do not need to send any update messages.

Pros:

- Use Less Bandwidth. (No bandwidth wastage for no movement)
- Scalability.

Cons:

- Flooding when there is no entry in location table cause congestion.
- Scalability is acting as drawback.
- Node periodically broadcast their physically address.
- Nearby nodes are updated more frequently as compare to far away nodes.
- Not suitable for large ad hoc networks.

16) GLS

Geographic Location Service (GLS) provides a distributed location service with large number of nodes. Nodes periodically exchange Hello messages with their neighbors. The Hello messages contain the sender's position and speed information. There are three main actions has been observed in GLS that is location server selection, location query request and location server update. When GLS want to forward packets, a mobile node consults its neighbor table and select the node closest to the destination and send it.

Pros:

- Traffic overhead is greatly reduced.
- GLS preserve the scalability of geographic forwarding.
- Scalability is acting as pros.
  Cons:

- Almost same disadvantages lie under the "cons" heading of Geographic Routing protocol.

17) CAR

Connectivity-Aware Routing (CAR) [47] designed specifically for inter-vehicle communication in a city and/or highway environment. In CAR once a path is found, it is auto-adjusted on the fly to account for changes, without another discovery process. "Guards" help to track the current position of a destination, even if it travels a substantial distance from its initially known location. CAR consists of four main parts, destination location and path discovery, data packet forwarding along the found path, path maintenance with the help of guard, error recovery [47].

Pros:

- Provide scalability.
- Generates less routing overhead traffic.

- Maximize the chance of successful delivery, because it adapts to current conditions to find a route with sufficient connectivity.
- Not only to locate positions of destinations but also to find connected path between source and destination pairs.
- Route maintenance is organized with the help of guard so route changes are corrected on the fly.

Cons:

- Increase network congestion because using periodic HELLO beacons information about their moving directions.
- Bandwidth wastage.
- Delaying of data packets.

Multi-Path

18) MLAR:

Multipath Location Based Routing (MLAR) This Algorithm uses a 3D approach particularly a hybrid extension to LAR that works in 3D. MLAR tries to reduce the protocol overhead by using two strategies. The first strategy limits the transmission area thus reducing the number of nodes participating in the forwarding of the route request packets. Only the nodes in the box region will participate in forwarding, others just discard the route request packet they received. The second strategy makes use of multiple alternative paths to reduce the number of consecutive routing requests in case the first one fails. The alternative paths can be tried for sending the packet if the first priority path does not work.

Pros:

- Improve Bandwidth when compare with LAR
- Propose Replacing LAR with Multipath LAR (MLAR) in GRID.
- Reduce the Protocol overhead.
- Provide scalability.

Cons:

- Out of Order Deliver Packets (Packets Reordering)
- Packet header contains entire source route
- Large Memory Required.
- Limited Bandwidth.

19) DA-MLAR-ODTP:

Directional Antenna Multipath Location Aided Routing with On Demand Transmission Power (DA-MLAR-ODTP) [49] is the more enhance version of MLAR. Directional Antenna model has been implemented in DA-MLAR to provide directional capability. Using the directional antenna in DA-MLAR provides longer transmission range. The network partition that could have happened using an omni-directional antenna has been avoided by using the directional antenna. There are two major problems exist in MLAR.

One problem with MLAR is that even when some nodes are not in the box region and they do not participate in forwarding the route request packet to the destination, they are still affected as they are within the communication radio range of the sender node. Second problem is that there are more cases of network partitions compared to DA-MLAR.

The energy distribution in directions other than the intended directions, not only causes interference to other nodes, but also reduces the potential range of transmission due to lower signal strength and multi-path components. With DA-MLAR within the request zone itself it is possible to involve only those intermediate nodes that are in the direction of destination from the source.

On demand transmission power modes are used while sending the packets and re-broadcasting after getting the error message. Keeping the antenna in default transmission power mode in all other times except for sending the packets and re-broadcasting after getting the error message. During those operations three transmission modes are used based on the calculated distance between the current sending node and the next hop node – low transmission mode, default transmission mode, and high transmission mode. This on demand transmission power strategy implemented for DA-MLAR will avoid excessive interference in a shared medium and also reduces the number of network partitioning

Pros:

- Provide lower overhead.
- Better network utilization.
- Better connectivity.
- Short end-to-end delay.
- Packet delivery ratio is increased.

Cons:

- Packet reordering occur because of multipath property.

POWER AWARE ROUTING PROTOCOL

Ad hoc nodes are operated by battery and have limited energy resources, because a node in an ad hoc network is typically a laptop, a personal digital assistant or any mobile device, energy supplied by batteries is likely to be a scarce resource, and in some applications energy is entirely non-renewable [50], make energy efficiency a key concern in the operation of such networks specially during wireless connectivity. Furthermore the lifetime of batteries has not been improved as fast as processing speed of microprocessors. In MANET the node consume more energy as compare to other wireless network because of absence of network infrastructure. Mobile node in MANET must act as a router and join in the process of packets forwarding so packets loads are high. Now we will discuss power management schemes Figure 1.

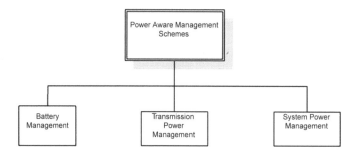

Fig.1. Provides an overview of the power aware management scheme.

Battery Management: The challenge is not to provide each node with higher battery power but to utilize the available battery power in a very efficient manner.

Transmission Power Management: Find out the minimum power limitation route. Find out the maximum average power route.

System Power Management: Find out the ways to minimize the power consumption during the processing task.

Power Aware Multi Access protocol with signaling ad hoc network (PAMAS) [51] is the main power aware protocol lies under the single path category the other protocol of the same category is Energy Efficient Unified Routing (EURo) [52] whereas Multipath Power Sensitive Routing Protocol (MPSR) [53] is used for multipath.

Pros:

- Minimize the power consumption in standby mode and communication mode.
- Network is more stable for long time.
- Every Node in the network is treated equally.

Cons:

- This method induces a delay for each transmission.
- No relevance for energy network powered transmission operated via sufficient repeater infrastructure.

Single Path

20) PAMAS:

The Power Aware Multi Access protocol (PAMAS) protocol is a combination of the original MACA protocol [54] and the idea of using a separate signaling channel as in [55][56]. Thus, we assume that the RTS-CTS message exchange takes place over a signaling channel that is separate from the channel used for packet transmissions. This separate signaling channel enables nodes to determine when and for how long they can power themselves off

Pros:

- PAMAS can save energy by shutting down radios.
- Increase time to network partition and reduce variation in node costs.

Cons:

- Do not know entire packet transmission path.
- More traffic congested.
- Load balancing is difficult.

21) EURo:

In practice, three key elements of transmission power, interference, and residual battery energy plan an important role in choosing energy-efficient routes. Previous studies [57][58] [59][60] have ignored one or more of these metrics, so Energy Efficient Unified Routing (EURo) [52] takes into accounts all of these critical metrics.

Pros:

- More energy efficient using all these approach.
  - o Transmission Power.
  - o Interference.
  - o Residual energy.
- Easy to implement.

Cons:

- End to end delay increased.
- More memory is required because it use Dijkstra's algorithm or Bellman-Ford Algorithm to find a minimum cost route.

Multi-Path

22) MPSR:

 Multipath Power Sensitive Routing Protocol (MPSR) shows how an efficient heuristic-based multipath technique can improve the meantime-to-node-failure and maintain the variance in the power of all the nodes as low as possible. The Routing table is constructed based on the weight (remaining power). The path having the maximum average power and minimum hop count is selected. MPSR is a flat topology in which every node is treated equally and stability and end-to-end.

Here we assume a non-hostile environment in which the nodes relay their original weights. A counter called route count (rCount) is maintained. This specifies the maximum number of routes that can be cached for a particular destination.

Pros:

- Improve the mean time to node failure.
- Maintain the variance in the power of all the nodes as low as possible.
- Every node in the network is treated equally.
- Overall network is stable for long time.
- End-to-end delay does not increase significantly.
- Use Less Bandwidth.

Cons:

- Delay for each transmission because at the destination node average power of each path is calculated..
- Very Difficult to Load balancing.
- Reliability is increased.

MULTICASTING ROUTING PROTOCOL

Now-a-days there are so many applications which can send data from one source node to selective nodes instead of broadcasting. Multicasting is the transmission of datagrams to a group of hosts identified by a single destination address [62].There are two major types of structure are used in multicasting whether in Tree based or Meshed based. Both structures have their own advantages and disadvantages. We are not going to discuss their pros and cons but to focus on their ways of transmitting data. The best suitable place for multicasting is in classroom or in military battlefield. Multicast Protocol for Mobile Ad hoc Network (MAODV) [63] and other popular protocol of single path is On-demand Multicast Routing Protocol ODMRP [64] where as Multi-flow Real-time Transport Protocol MRTP [65] are the category of multipath protocols. The main pros and cons of multicasting protocols are

Pros:

- Useful when broadcasting to specific nodes only.
- Multicast Routing protocols are energy savers.
- Save Bandwidth.
- Minimize sender and router processing.
- Minimize delivery delay.
- Reduce the communication cost for applications that send the same data to multiple recipients.

Cons:

- More Memory Required.
- More Congested.

Single Path

23) MAODV:

The Multicast Ad-hoc On-Demand Distance Vector (MAODV) routing protocol discovers multicast routes on demand using a broadcast route-discovery mechanism. It almost follows the same procedure of AODV but providing the extra functionality of multicasting. It use the same procedure of RREQ and RREP initialize the connection among the nodes. MAODV shared bi-directional multicast tree.

Pros:

- Efficient Algorithm
- Loop free Algorithm.
- More Efficient because of bi-directional characteristics.

- Avoids sending duplicate packets to the receivers.

Cons:

- If an intermediate node on the path moves away , the reply is lost because of MAODV unicast the reply back to source.

24) ODMRP:

On-demand Multicast Routing Protocol (ODMRP) maintains a mesh topology, uses forwarding group concept that is only a subset of nodes forward multicast packets. No explicit control message is required to leave the group. When a multicast source has packets to send, but no route to the multicast group, it broadcasts a Join-Query control packet to the entire network. This Join-Query packet is periodically broadcast to refresh the membership information and update routes.

Pros:

- Sender Forms and Maintains the multicast group
- Richer connectivity (multiple routes for one particular destination)
- High packet delivery ratio.
  Cons:

- Control overhead of route refreshes (scalability issue).
- Extra processing overhead because of broadcasting reply back to source.
- Global Flooding of the Join Request
- Congested traffic.

Multi-Path

25) MRTP:

Multi-flow Real-time Transport Protocol (MRTP) is Mesh Based protocol for multipath in ad-hoc networks. It Provides a convenient vehicle for real time applications to partition and transmit data using multiple flows. Ad hoc based protocol offer multipath routing for multicast application provides a framework for applications to transmit real time data. The transport service provided by MRTP is end-to-end using the association of multiple flows.

Pros:

- Best suitable for multimedia applications.
- Improve the queuing performance by using partitioning techniques such as striping and thinning.

Cons:

- High processing is required.
- Delay is observed because reordering of the packets base on timestamp is required.

ADAPTIVE ROUTING

Adaptive routing protocol combines the advantages of proactive and of reactive routing. The routing is initially established with some proactively prospected routes and then serves the demand from additionally activated nodes through reactive flooding. Temporally Ordered

Routing Algorithm (TORA) [66], [67] is the single path protocol. In case of multi-path Multipath Temporally Ordered Routing Algorithm (M-TORA) [68] is used.

Pros:

- Memory efficient.
- Improve scalability.
- Because of reactive nature hosts can quickly obtain route information.
- Reliable.

Cons:

- Advantage depends on amount of nodes activated.
- Reaction to traffic demand depends on gradient of traffic volume.
- End to end delay increased.
- Bandwidth wastage because of flooding

Single Path

26) TORA:

Temporally Ordered Routing Algorithm (TORA) [66], [67] is based on the concept of link reversal. It is reactive routing protocol. TORA improves the partial link reversal method by detecting partitions and stopping non-productive link reversals. TORA can be used for highly dynamic mobile ad hoc networks. In TORA, the network topology is regarded as a directed graph. TORA has three basic operations: route creation, route maintenance and route erasure. A route creation operation starts with setting the height (propagation ordering parameter in the quintuple) of the destination to 0 and heights of all other nodes to NULL (i.e., undefined). The source broadcasts a QRY packet containing the destination's ID. A node with a non-NULL height responds by broadcasting a UPD packet containing the height of its own. On receiving a UPD packet, a node sets its height to one more than that of the UPD generator. A node with higher height is considered as upstream and the node with lower height is considered as downstream. In this way, a directed acyclic graph (DAG) is constructed from the source to the destination and multiple paths route may exist. TORA can create and maintain multiple paths to destination.

Pros:

- Loop free route.
- Reduce the effect of congested traffic.
- Can be used for highly dynamic mobile ad hoc networks.

Cons:

- Node re-constructs DAG when it lost all downstream links. So delay is increased.
- Increase complexity because all nodes must have synchronize clock.

Multi-Path

27) M-TORA:

The basic idea of Multipath Temporally Ordered Routing Algorithm (M-TORA) [68] is to present a new routing path selection strategy which takes into account of not only hop count but also the packet queue length in MAC layer. In this way M-TORA can sufficiently make use of the multiple paths.

The modifications based on TORA are on two aspects: adding new items in Internet MANET Encapsulation Protocol (IMEP) control packet header field and modifying the selections strategy in classical TORA protocol.

IMEP is a multipurpose network-layer encapsulation protocol designed for MANET. It supports the operations of many routing algorithms, network control protocols and other Upper Layer Protocols (ULP). ULP packets can be encapsulated into IMEP packets. IMEP and TORA have been designed to work together synergistically. With the support of IMEP, TORA achieves multi-hop distributed routing, multi-path support and route cycle avoidance.

Pros:

- Decreasing packet end-to-end delay. Especially in high traffic load.
- Loading balancing.
- Improve packet delivery ratio.
- Reduce the possibility that packet destroyed caused by network congestion.
- Energy consumption in network is more fairly distributed.
  Cons:

- Complexity difficult to implement.
- Network energy consumption is higher especially in high load traffic.
- Spending more energy because not always forward the packet over the shortest known path.

CONCLUSION

Routing is an essential component of communication protocol in mobile ad hoc networks. In this paper, the effect of single path and multi path routing protocols in MANET has been investigated. These protocols performance enhancement are observed. The best routing protocol can be selected as per particular environment and needs. Taxonomy of described MANET routing schemes is given in Table 1. The survey tries to review typical routing protocols and reveals the characteristics and trade-off.

Experimental design, physical requirements and QoS are not included in this survey.

Many researchers proposed their schemes to solve the limitation problems discussed in Section I. The design of MANET routing protocols includes node mobility that causes frequent topology changes and network partitions, secondly due to variable and unpredictable capacity of wireless links, packet losses may happen frequently in MANET. Moreover, the broadcast nature of wireless medium introduces the hidden terminal and exposed terminal problems. This report gives the current review for typical routing protocols not only for the uni-path protocols but also focuses and points out the main pros and cons of each multi-path protocol. We analyze the result based on the classification methods.

We also present and compare the main characteristics of different protocols among themselves which can be clearly shown in the Table1.

Nanotechnology and miniaturized devices require less power to operate. These devices require more power for wireless connectivity. The usage of such devices is on high demand hence requiring more protection to user data that can be achieved by enhancing security-aware-protocol. Further research is needed to identify the best security aware and energy efficient based routing protocols for various network contexts.

Improvement relying on single layer cannot entirely solve all the existing problems. All protocols ranging from physical to application layers need to be improved or re-invented.

Another research direction is to provide the secure path to the route. Advanced statistical methods or machine learning algorithms may be used for this. The mechanisms for the security protocols should operate on an end-to-end basis and should not impose much computational burden on the host nodes.

Table 1. Comparing the different Characteristics of Routing Protcols of MANET

Protocols	Structure	Loop-Free	Updates transmitted to	Route Metrics	Utilize Hello Messages
DSDV	Proactive	Yes	Neighbors	Shortest Path	Yes
WRP	Proactive	Yes, but not instantaneous	Neighbors	Shortest Path	Yes
MDSDV	Proactive	Yes	Neighbors	Shortest Path	Yes
TERA	Proactive	Yes	Neighbors	Shortest Path	Yes
DSR	Reactive	Yes	Neighbors	Shortest Path	No
AODV	Reactive	Yes	Neighbors	Freshest and Shortest Path	Yes
MSR	Reactive	Yes	Neighbors	Depends (Takes multiple paths)	No
AOMDV	Reactive	Yes	Neighbors	Depends (Takes multiple paths)	Yes
ZRP	Hybrid	Yes	Neighbors	First Inside then outside the zone	Yes
AntHocNet	Hybrid/proactive	Yes	Neighbors	Depends (Takes multiple paths)	Yes
HSR	Hybrid	Yes	Cluster and Cluster Head	Shortest Path	No
CBRP	Reactive	Yes	Neighbors and Cluster Head	First available Route	No
HMFR	Hierarchical/hybrid	No	Neighbors	Depends (Takes multiple paths)	No
LAR	Reactive	No	Location based sending	GPS Based	No
DREAM	Proactive	Yes	Location based sending	GPS Based	No
GLS	Proactive	Yes	Location based sending	GPS Based	Yes
CAR	Proactive	Yes	Location based sending	GPS Based	Yes
MLAR	Proactive	No	Location based sending	GPS Based	Yes
DA-MLAR-ODTP	Proactive	No	Location based sending	GPS Based	No
PAMAS	Depend	Depend (where it used)	Depend (where it used)	Power Efficient Based	Depend (where it used)
EURo	Reactive	No	Neighbors	Shortest Path and Power save	No
MPSR	Depend (where it used)	Depend (where it used)	Depend (where it used)	Energy Efficient Based	Depend (where it used)
MAODV	Reactive	Yes	Neighbors	Shortest Path to each node	Yes
ODMRP	Reactive	Yes	Neighbors	Shortest Path	Yes
MRTP	Reacive	Yes	Neighbors	Depends (Takes multiple paths)	Yes
TORA	Reactive	Yes	Neighbors	Shortest Path	No
M-TORA	Reactive	Yes	Neighbors	Depends (Takes multiple paths)	No

Protocols	Memory Required	Route Maintained In	Scalability	Route Availability	Frequency of Updates
DSDV	Normal	Route Table	Good	Available	Periodic
WRP	High	Route Table	Fair	Available	Periodic
MDSDV	Normal	Route Table	Good	Available	Periodic
TERA	High	Route Table	Good	Available	Periodic
DSR	Low	Route Cache	Bad	Available	Not Periodic
AODV	Low	Route Table	Good	Determined when needed	Not periodic
MSR	Low	Route Cache	Bad	Determined when needed	Not Periodic
AOMDV	Low	Route Table	Good	Determined when needed	Not Periodic
ZRP	Normal	Intrazone and Inerzone tables	Fair	Depend on Location of the destination	Periodic
AntHocNet	Normal	Route Table	Good	Available	Periodic
HSR	High	Route Table and Cluster Head	Fair	Determined when needed	Periodic
CBRP	Normal	Route Table and Cluster Head	Fair	Determined when needed	Not Periodic
HMFR	High	Route Table	Good	Determined when needed	-
LAR	High	Route Table	Good	Determined when needed	Not Periodic Mobility Based
DREAM	High	Route Table	Good	Available	Periodic Mobility Based
GLS	High	Route Table	Good	Available	Periodic Mobility Based
CAR	High	Route Table	Good	Available	Periodic Mobility Based
MLAR	High	Route Table	Good	Available	Periodic Mobility Based
DA-MLAR-ODTP	High	Route Table	-	Available	Periodic Mobility Based
PAMAS	Depend (where it used)	Depend (where it used)	Depend (where it used)	Depend (where it used)	Depend (where it used)
EURo	High	Route Cache	-	Determined when needed	Periodic
MPSR	-	Routing Table	Good	Depend (where it used)	Depend (where it used)
MAODV	Low	Route Table	Good	Determined when needed	Not Periodic
ODMRP	High	Route Cache	Fair	Determined when needed	Not Periodic
MRTP	Normal	Route Cache	Fair	Depend (where it used)	Not Periodic
TORA	High	Route Table	Good	Determined when needed	Not Periodic
M-TORA	High	Route Table	Good	Determined when needed	Not Periodic

REFERENCES

[1]   Internet Engineering Task Force (IETF) Mobile Ad Hoc Networks (MANET) Working Group Charter, http://www.ietf.org/html.charters/manet-charter.html.

[2]   Charles E. Perkins, *Ad Hoc Networking*, Pearson Education, New Jersey, USA (2000).

[3]   Izhak Rubin Y.-C. Liu, *Link Stability Models for QoS Ad Hoc Routing Algorithms*, In Proceedings of Vehicular Technology Conference, 2003. VTC 2003, IEEE 58th Volume 5, Oct. 2003 pp. 3084 – 3088.

[4]   S. Mueller, D. Ghosal, *Multipath routing in mobile ad hoc networks: issues and challenges*, Lecture Notes in Computer Science, 2004.

[5]   N. F. Maxemchuk, *Diversity Routing*, In Proc. IEEE ICC, San Francisco, CA, 1975.

[6]   J. Chen, S.Chan, and V.Li, *Multipath routing for video delivery over bandwidth-limited networks,*" IEEE JSAC, 2004.

[7]   A. Elwalid, C. Jin, S. Low, and I. Widjaja, *MATE: MPLS adaptive traffic engineering*, in Proc. of INFOCOM, 2001.

[8]   V. Mirrokni, M. Thottan, H. Uzunalioglu, and S. Paul, *Simple polynomial time frameworks for reduced-path decomposition in multi-path routing*, in Proceedings of IEEE INFOCOM, 2004.

[9]   S. J. Lee and M. Gerla, *Split multipath routing with maximally disjoint paths in ad hoc networks,*" in Proc. of ICC, 2001.

[10]   S. Bohacek, J. Hespanha, J. Lee, K. Obraczka, and C. Lim, *Enhancing security via stochastic routing*, in Proc. of the 11th IEEE Int. Conf. On Computer. Communications and Networks, 2002.

[11]   P. Papadimitratos and Z. Haas, *Secure data transmission in mobile ad hoc networks*, In Proc of the 2nd ACM workshop on Wireless security, San Diego, CA, USA,2003,pp. 41 - 50.

[12]   P. Lee, V. Misra, and D. Rubenstein, *Distributed algorithms for secure multipath routing*, in Proc. of INFOCOM, Mar. 2005.

[13]   S. Bohacek, J. Hespanha, J. Lee, C. Lim, and K. Obraczka, *Game theoretic stochastic routing*, Submitted, 2005.

[14]   M. Marina and S. Das, "On-demand multipath distance vector routing in ad hoc networks," in Proc. of ICNP, 2001.

[15]   C. Tang and P. K. McKinley, *A distributed multipath computation framework for overlay network applications*, tech. rep., Michigan State University, 2004.

[16]   Charles Perkins and Pravin Bhagwat, "*Highly Dynamic Destination-Sequenced Distance-Vector Routing for Mobile Computers*", In Proceedings of the Symposium on Communication Architectures and Protocols, ACM SIGCOMM, 1994

[17]   Shree Murthy, J.J. Garcia-Luna-Aveces *A Routing Protocol for Packet Radio Networks*, Proc. ACM International Conference on Mobile Computing and Networking, November, 1995, pp. 86-95.

[18]   Dr Peter J.B King, Ali A. Etorban, Idris Skloul Ibrahim "*A DSDV-based Multipath Routing Protocol for Mobile Ad-Hoc Networks*", Proceedings of 8th Annual Postgraduate Symposium on The Convergence of Telecommunications, Networking and Broadcastig, Jones Moores University, UK, 2007

[19]   Ralph Jansen, Sven Hanemann and Bernd Freisleben, "*Proactive Distance-Vector Multipath Routing for Wireless Ad Hoc Networks*", Proceedings of 10th Symposium on Communicati-ons and Vehicular Technology, Eindhoven, Netherlands, SCVT 2003

[20]   C. Hedrick. Routing Information Protocol. RFC 1058, June 1988.

[21]   Per Johansson and Tony Larsson and Nicklas Hedman and Bartosz Mielczarek and Mikael Degermark *Scenario-based Performance Analysis of Routing Protocols for Mobile Ad-hoc Networks* Proceedings of the 5th annual ACM/IEEE international conference on Mobile computing and networking, Seattle, Washington, United States, MobiCom '1999, pp. 195-206.

[22]   Murthy, S. and J.J. Garcia-Luna-Aceves, "*An Efficient Routing Protocol for Wireless Networks*", ACM Mobile Networks and App. J., Special Issue on Routing in Mobile Communication Networks, Oct. 1996, pp. 183-97.

[23]   A.S. Tanenbaum, Computer Networks, 3rd ed., Ch. 5, Englewood Cliffs,NJ: Prentice Hall, 1996, pp. 357–58.

[24]   Royer, E.M.; Chai-Keong Toh, "*A review of current routing protocols for ad hoc mobile wireless networks*", Personal Communications, IEEE Volume 6, April 1999 pp. 46 – 55

[25]   Ralph Jansen and Bernd Freisleben. *Bandwidth efficient distant vector routing for ad hoc networks*. In Proceedings of the Wireless and Optical Communications Conference (WOC), pages 117–122, Banff, Canada, June 2001. IASTED, Iasted-Acta Press.

[26]   David Johnson, David Maltz, Yih-Chun Hu*: The Dynamic Source Routing Protocol for Mobile Ad Hoc Networks for IPv4*, RFC 4728

[27]   David B. Johnson, David A. Maltz*: "Dynamic Source Routing in Ad Hoc Wireless Network"s,* Mobile Computing, Thomasz Imielinski and Hank Korth (Editors), Vol. 353, Chapter 5, pp. 153-181, Kluwer Academic Publishers, 1996

[28]   C. Perkins, E. Belding-Royer *Ad hoc On-Demand Distance Vector (AODV) Routing*. RFC 3561, July 2003.

[29]   Lei Wang, Lianfang Zhang, Yantai Shu and Miao Dong, "*Multipath Source Routing in Wireless Ad Hoc Networks*", CCECE 2000, 7-10 March 2000.

[30]   M. Marina, S. Das: "*On-demand Multipath Distance Vector Routing in Ad Hoc Networks*", Proceedings of the 2001 IEEE International Conference on Network Protocols (ICNP), IEEE Computer Society Press, 2001 pp. 14-23.

[31]   C. E. Perkins and E. M. Royer, "*Ad-hoc On-Demand Distance Vector Routing*," Proc. 2nd IEEE Wksp. Mobile Comp. Sys. and Apps., Feb. 1999, pp. 90–100.

[32]   Mehran Abolhasan, Tadeusz Wysocki, Eryk Dutkiewicz, *A review of routing protocols for mobile ad hoc networks* Ad Hoc Networks, Volume 2, Issue 1, January 2004, pp. 1-22

[33]   Zygmunt J. Haas, Marc R. Pearlman, Prince Samar *"The Zone Routing Protocol (ZRP) for Ad Hoc Networks"*, Internet Draft, July 2002

[34]   Frederick Ducatelle, Gianni Di Caro and Luca Maria Gambardella, *"Ant Agents for Hybrid Multipath Routing in Mobile Ad Hoc Networks"*, Wireless Ondemand Network Systems and Services, 2005. WONS 2005. Jan. 2005

[35]   Maekawa, T.; Tada, H.; Wakamiya, N.; Imase, M.; Murata, M.; *"An Ant-based Routing Protocol using Unidirectional Links for Heterogeneous Mobile Ad-Hoc Networks"* Wireless and Mobile Communications, 2006. ICWMC '06. July 2006 pp.43-50

[36]   G. Pei, M. Gerla, X. Hong, C. Chiang, *A wireless hierarchical routing protocol with group mobility*, in: Proceedings of Wireless Communications and Networking, New Orleans, 1999.

[37]   John M. McQuillan, Isaac Richer and Eric C. Rosen, *ARPANet Routing Algorithm Improvements*, BBN Report No. 3803, Cambridge, April 1978

[38]   A. Iwata, C.-C. Chiang, G. Pei, M. Gerla, and T.-W. Chen, *Scalable routing strategies for ad hoc wireless networks*. IEEE Journal on Selected Areas in Communications, Special Issue on Ad-Hoc Networks, August 1999, p1369-p1379.

[39]   M. JIANG, J. LI, Y. C. TAY *Cluster Based Routing Protocol* (CBRP) Functional Specification Internet Draft, draft-ietf-manet-cbrp.txt, work in progress, June 1999.

[40]   Chansook Lim Bohacek, S. Hespanha, J.P. Obraczka, K. *Hierarchical max-flow routing"*, In proceedings of the Global Telecommunications Conference, GLOBECOM '05. 28 Nov, Volume: 1, On page(s): 6 pp

[41]   Stephan Bohacek, Joòao P. Hespanha, Chansook Lim, Katia Obraczka, *"Hierarchical Max-Flow Routing"*, To be presented at the 2005 IEEE GLOBECOM, Nov. 2005

[42]   G. G. Finn, *Routing and Addressing Problems in Large Metropolitan-Scale Internetworks*, ISI res. rep. ISU/RR- 87-180, Mar. 1987.

[43]   Prosenjit Bose, Pat Morin, Ivan Stojmenovic, and Jorge Urrutia. *Routing with guaranteed delivery in ad hoc wireless networks*. In 3rd Workshop on Discrete Algorithms and Methods for Mobile Computing and Communication (DIALM '99), pages 48–55,1999.

[44]   Y. B. Ko and N. H. Vaidya. *Location Aid Routing (LAR) in mobile ad hoc networks*. In Proc. ACM/IEEE MOBICOM, Oct. 1998..

[45]   S. Basagni, I. Chlamtac, V. R. Syrotiuk, B. A. Woodward *A Distance Routing Effect Algorithm for Mobility (DREAM)* In Proc. ACM/IEEE Mobicom, pages 76-84, October 1998.

[46]   Inyang Li, john Janotti, Douglas S. J. De Coutu, David R. Karger, Robert Morris *A Scalable Location Service for Geographic Ad Hoc Routing* In Proc. MOBICOM'2000, Boston, MA, USA, 2000.

[47]   Naumov, V. Gross, T.R Connectivity-Aware Routing (CAR) in Vehicular Ad-hoc Networks, In Proceeding of 26th IEEE International Conference on Computer Communications, INFOCOM 2007, Anchorage, AK, May 2007, pp. 1919 – 1927.

[48]   Soumendra Nanda, Robert S. Gray, *Spatial Multipath Location Aided Ad Hoc Routing*, Computer Communications and Networks, 2004. ICCCN 2004. Proceedings. 13th International Conference on 2004.

[49]   Gajurel, S. Malakooti, B. Limin Wang, *DA-MLAR-ODTP: Directional Antenna Multipath Location Aided Routing with On Demand Transmission Power* In Proc. Wireless Pervasive Computing, 2007. ISWPC '07. 2nd International Symposium, April , 2007.

[50]   Anthony Ephremides, *Energy concerns in wireless networks*, IEEE Wireless Communications 9 (4) (2002), pp. 48–59.

[51]   S. SINGH, C.S. RAGHAVENDRA PAMAS & *PAMAS-Power Aware Multi Access Protocol with Signaling Ad Hoc Networks,* ACM SIGCOMM Computer Communication Review Volume 28 , July 1998, pp. 5 – 26.

[52]   Sungoh Kwon Shroff, N.B., *Unified Energy-Efficient Routing for Multi-Hop Wireless Networks* Proceedings of INFOCOM 2008. The 27th Conference on Computer Communications. IEEE, April 2008, pp. 430 – 438.

[53]   Ralph Jansen, Sven Hanemann and Bernd Freisleben, *Proactive Distance-Vector Multipath Routing for Wireless Ad Hoc Networks*, Proceedings of 10th Symposium on Communicati-ons and Vehicular Technology, Eindhoven, Netherlands, SCVT 2003.

[54]   P. Karn,*MACA - a New Channel Access Method for Packet Radio*, in ARRL/CRRL Amateur Radio 9th Computer Networking Conference, pp. 134-140, 1990.

[55]   Cheng-shong Wu and Victor O.K. Li, *Receiver-Initiated Busy-Tone Multiple Access in Packet Radio Networks*, Proceedings ACM SIGCOMM'87 Workshop, Stowe, Vermont, Aug. 11-15, Vol. 17(5), pp. 336-342, 1987

[56]   F. A. Tobagi and L. Kleinrock, *Packet Switching in radio channels: Part II - the hidden terminal problem in carrier sense multiple-access modes and the busy-tone solution*", IEEE Trans. Communications, Vol. COM- 23(12), 1975, pp. 1417-1433.

[57]   T. Melodia, D. Pompili, and I. F. Akyildiz, *Optimal local topology knowledge for energy efficient geographical routing in sensor networks*, in *IEEE INFOCOM'04*, March 2004, vol. 3, pp. 1705–1716.

[58]   R. Manohar and A. Scaglione, *Power optimal routing in wireless Networks,* in *IEEE International Conference on Communications (ICC)'03*, May 2003, vol. 4, pp. 2979–2984.

[59]   H. Wei, S. Ganguly, R. Izmailov, and Z. J. Hass, *Interference-aware IEEE 802.16 wimax mesh networks*, in *IEEE VTC'05-Spring*, May-June, 2005, vol. 5, pp. 3102 – 3106

[60]   J. Tang, G. Xue, C. Chandler, and W. Zhang, *Interference-aware routing in multihop wireless networks using directional antennas,"* in *IEEE INFOCOM'05*, March 2005, vol. 1, pp. 751–260

[61]   W. Lou and Y. Fang. *A Survey of Wireless Security in Mobile Ad Hoc Networks: Challenges and Available Solutions*. In X. Huang X. Cheng and D. Z. Du, editors, Ad Hoc Wireless Networking. Kluwer, May 2003.

[62] S. Deering, *Host extensions for IP multicasting*, RFC 1112, August 1989, available at http://www.ietf.org/rfc/rfc1112.txt

[63] E. Royer, and C. E. Perkins *Multicast operation of the ad-hoc on-demand distance vector routing protocol*, Proc. of the 5th ACM/IEEE Annual Conf. on Mobile Computing and Networking, Aug. 1999, pp. 207-218.

[64] Sung-Ju Lee, Mario Gerla, and Ching-Chuan Chiang: *On-Demand Multicast Routing Protocol*, In Proc. of the Wireless Communications and Networking Conference (WCNC), New Orleans, LA, September 1999, pp. 1298 – 1302.

[65] Shiwen Mao, Dennis Bushmitch, Sathya Narayanan, and Shivendra S. Panwar, *MRTP: A Multi-Flow Realtime Transport Protocol for Ad Hoc Networks*, Vehicular Technology Conference, 2003, 6-9 Oct. 2003

[66] V. D. Park and M. S. Corson. *A highly adaptive distributed routing algorithm for mobile wireless networks*, INFOCOM '97, 16th Annual Joint Conference of the IEEE Computer and Communications Societies. Proceedings IEEE, Volume: 3, 1997 pp. 1405 -1413 vol.3.

[67] V. Park, and S. Corson, *Temporally-Ordered Routing Algorithm (TORA)* Version 1 Functional Specification. IETF Internet draft, 1997.

[68] Liu, Qiang Wang, Hua Kuang, Jingming Wang, Zheng Bi, Zhiming *M-TORA: a TORA-Based Multi-Path Routing Algorithm for Mobile Ad Hoc Networks*, In proceeding of Global Telecommunications Conference, 2006. GLOBECOM '06. IEEE, Location: San Francisco, CA, USA, Nov. 2006, pp. 1 – 5.

## CHAPTER 2

Development of Distance Computing Environment for Parallel Processing

Syed Misbahuddin and Fazal Noor

Department of Computer Science and Software Engineering, University of Hail, Saudi Arabia

Abstract: Parallel processing is a form of computing in which a number of activities are carried out concurrently on multiple machines so that the time required to solve a given problem is reduced. The advent of low cost high performance Pentium machines and PC based LINUX operating system have attracted many researchers to explore parallel processing experiments on PCs. This chapter provides the complete experience of building a LINUX cluster and its application in mapping some parallel algorithms. This chapter discusses comprehensive procedure of cluster development. It discusses the procedure of linear expansion of a cluster to *n* nodes. Furthermore, the chapter describes the experience of replacing an existing node if it either fails or needs to be replaced by another powerful node.

INTRODUCTION

Supercomputers have been used in many parallel computing applications solving very complex problems. However, their popularity is declining due to several factors such as high capital cost for both software and hardware. Parallel processing is also possible by making a cluster of Intel based low cost personal computers [1]. This chapter describes the experience of making a cluster utilizing low cost Pentium machines and network infrastructure. We will discuss the cluster utilization from various simple scientific applications [2]. Furthermore, this chapter discusses the planning and implementation of remote access developed cluster via Internet or corporate Intranet infrastructure. This facility will help the scientific community to run their parallel jobs on the cluster from any place. The chapter is organized as follows: in section 2, brief introduction to parallel programming rationale is discussed. Section 3 describes step-by-step Cluster development process. Cluster utilization for implementing parallel applications, is elaborated in section 4. Remote access of the cluster is discussed in section 5. The conclusion is given in section 6. Finally, step by step process of developing Intel PC based parallel processing platform has been described in the Appendix at the end of this chapter.

PARALLEL PROGRAMMING

Parallel Programming is used to improve computational speed of a given problem. The demand for increased computational power is increasing day by day. Several areas could be identified where faster computers are required such as weather forecasting, numerical simulation of engineering and scientific problems, modeling large DNA structures etc. In order to accommodate computationally fast algorithms, parallel or fast computers are needed. If a parallel computer is used, parallel programming techniques are used in which a given problem is decomposed into n independent segments and then submitted to *n* CPU's for execution concurrently as shown in Figure 1.

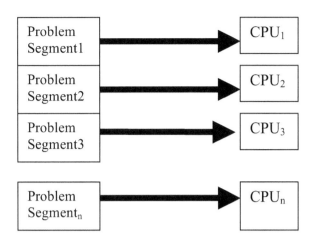

Fig. 1. Problem distribution for Parallel programming

In parallel programming software, the mechanism should be available to distribute the tasks among independent processors. Process coordination by message passing is required to achieve the problem solution objective. Advanced developers have designed and implemented several interesting programming models to help develop parallel applications. The most popular ones are OpenMP for shared memory programming and MPI (Message Passing Interface) for distributed memory **multi computer Architectures** [3][4]. There are several MPI implementations such as MPICH[5], LAM[6], Common High-level Interface to Message-Passing CHIMP[7] etc. In this chapter the emphasis is on LAM implementation. Local Area Multicomputer (LAM) was developed at Ohio Supercomputer Center. LAM is a programming environment and development system for message-passing heterogeneous parallel LINUX machines on a network. Using LAM, a LINUX cluster can act as one parallel computer solving one compute-intensive problem.

DEVELOPMENT OF PC CLUSTER

This section describes the planning and implementation of a PC cluster. Initially, one can start out a cluster of 3 nodes (1 Server + 2 Nodes). Then the system can be built of any size by linear expanding of nodes one by one. Here the system is expanded linearly by adding 14 nodes to make a 17 nodes cluster (1 Server + 16 Nodes). This scheme allows one to make a Master-Worker model with one master and 16 workers. The number of worker nodes is kept even for the graceful mapping of parallel algorithms on the cluster. Figure 2 shows a 17 node cluster. In this cluster machine named S1 is a NFS/NIS server (master) and all other machines (S2 – S17) are NFS/NIS clients. NFS/NIS server machine works as master node and all NFS/NIS client machines work as worker nodes. To build this cluster, a mix of P3 and P4 machines are used producing a heterogeneous cluster. The cluster building steps are summarized below:

1) Installation of Linux Enterprise edition on all Pentium machines.

2) Network configuration on Linux nodes.

3) Configuring NFS/NIS server and nodes.

4) Configuring Local Area Multicomputer (LAM) environment for launching parallel applications on all Linux nodes.

Complete steps of building a cluster are given in the Appendix at the end of this chapter.

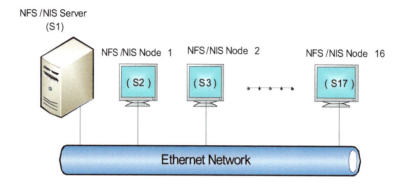

Fig. 2. LINUX PC Cluster of 17 nodes.

UTILIZING LINUX CLUSTER FOR PARALLEL PROCESSING

Parallel programs are executed on LINUX cluster by two methods:
1. Interactive: Users' programs are directly executed by the login shell and run immediately.
2. Batch: Users submit jobs to the system, which will be executed according to the available resources and site policy.

Here only the Interactive option is considered. In this method, a non-root user logs on the NFS server of the cluster locally or remotely and launches LAM parallel programming environment (PPE). The PPE can be established on all nodes in the cluster or on a subset of nodes depending upon the type of computation needed. To initiate PPE, participating nodes' host names are written in a text file and a command called "lamboot" is issued by on the NFS server. The syntax of initiated PPE is shown below:
        $lamboot –v machinefile

In the above command, "machinefile" is the text file containing the names of machines on which PPE is to be launched.   A parallel program can be written in C utilizing MPI functions. The parallel program will be compiled by a special compiler as follows:

        $mpicc –o programout program.c -lm

(Note: In above command, -lm option is to include math library during compilation)

The executable image can be sent to run on n nodes in the cluster by the following MPI command:

        $mpirun –np < executable image name>

Where *n* is the number of machines on which executable image will be executed. For example if the executable image name is "programout" and *n*=17, then the following command can be issued on the NFS server:

$mpirun –np 17 programout

The above command sets up seventeen separate instances of program out, one on each processor in the cluster.

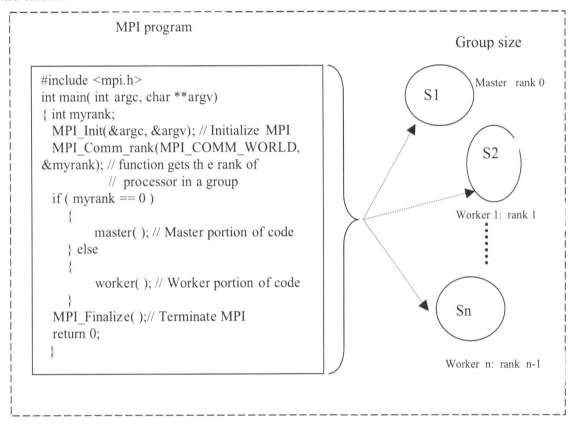

Fig. 3a. Each processor S1, S2, to Sn receives the code but only execute their portion depending on their rank in the group.

PROCESS CONTROL ON LINUX CLUSTER

The process control on a LINUX cluster is achieved by inserting MPI functions in the program. Table 1, lists some of the basic functions with their syntax. For example a typical parallel program will have MPI_Comm_rank(MPI_COMM_WORLD,&my_rank) inserted. This function returns an integer to the variable my_rank. The value of my_rank will be 0 for master, 1 for node 1, 2 for node 2 etc as in the order listed in the machinefile. As mpirun launches a copy of executable program on each node in the group of processors, selected portion(s) of the code gets executed by a particular node(s) by inserting conditional statements such as "if – else" statements with my_rank in the condition. This process control is shown in Figures 3a and 3b.

```
master( )
{
  MPI_Comm_size(MPI_COMM_WORLD, &nprocs); // Obtains number of processors

  for (rank = 1; rank < nprocs; ++rank)   // Dispatch to each processor a job
  {
    job = work_to_get_done();             // Obtain a job to send to processor

    MPI_Send(&job,1,MPI_INT,rank,JOBTAG,MPI_COMM_WORLD); // Send a job to
                                                          // processor
  }                                                       // with rank i

  job = work_to_get_done();  // Obtain another job to be given to a worker

  while (job != NULL)         // Use while loop to communicate back and forth
  {                           // between master and worker
      MPI_Recv(&result,1,MPI_DOUBLE,MPI_ANY_SOURCE,MPI_ANY_TAG,MPI_COMM_WORLD,&status)
      ; // Master is waiting for result from any worker who finished

      MPI_Send(&job,1,MPI_INT,status.MPI_SOURCE,JOBTAG,MPI_COMM_WORLD);
      // Dispatches another job to the same worker who recently sent a result

      job = work_to_get_done(); // Obtain another job to be given to worker
  }
  // No more jobs to give to workers therefore receive results to those
  // already being worked on by the workers.
  for (rank = 1; rank < nprocs; ++rank)
  {
      MPI_Recv(&result,1,MPI_DOUBLE,MPI_ANY_SOURCE,MPI_ANY_TAG,MPI_COMM_WORLD,&status)
      ; // Waits for results of outstanding jobs.
  }
  // Master sends signal to workers to indicate no more jobs therefore exit
  for (rank = 1; rank < nprocs; ++rank)
  {
    MPI_Send(0, 0, MPI_INT, rank, ENDTAG, MPI_COMM_WORLD);
  }
}

worker( )
{
    while (1)
  { // Worker waits to receive a job from master
    MPI_Recv(&job, 1, MPI_INT, 0, MPI_ANY_TAG,MPI_COMM_WORLD, &status);

    if (status.MPI_TAG == ENDTAG) // Tag indicates no more jobs, exit loop
    {
      return;
    }

    result = do_work(job); // function takes the job and gets the results
    // worker then sends the result back to master and loops waiting for more.
    MPI_Send(&result, 1, MPI_DOUBLE, 0, 0, MPI_COMM_WORLD);
  }
}
```

Fig. 3b. Master code portion is executed by the server and worker portion is executed by the node with messages being exchanged between master and workers.

Table 1: The six basic MPI functions used in writing MPI programs.

	Name	*Syntax*	*Function*

1	MPI_Init	`int MPI_Init(int *argc, char ***argv)`
		
		`Input: argc - Pointer to the number of arguments,     argv - Pointer to the argument vector`
			Initialize MPI

2	MPI_Comm_size	`int MPI_Comm_size(MPI_Comm comm, int *size)`
		
		`Input: comm - communicator (handle)`
		`Ouput: size - number of processes in the group of comm`
			Finds how many processes there are in the group

3	MPI_Comm_rank	`int MPI_Comm_rank(MPI_Comm comm, int *rank)`
		
		`Input:comm - communicator (handle),`
		
		`Output:rank - rank of the calling process in the group of comm (integer)`
			Finds which process number it is in the group

4	MPI_Send	`int MPI_Send(void* buf, int count,MPI_Datatype datatype, int dest,int tag, MPI_Comm comm)`
		
		`Input:buf - initial address of send buffer (choice), count - number of elements in send buffer (nonnegative integer), datatype - datatype of each send buffer element (handle), dest - rank of destination (integer), tag - message tag (integer), comm - communicator (handle)`
			Send a message

5	MPI_Recv	`int MPI_Recv(void* buf, int count, MPI_Datatype datatype, int source, int tag, MPI_Comm comm, MPI_Status *status)`
		
		`Output: buf - initial address of receive buffer, status - status object, provides information about message received; status is a structure of type MPI_Status, the element status.MPI_SOURCE is the source of the message received, and the element status.MPI_TAG is the tag value.`
		
		`Input: count - maximum number of elements in receive buffer (integer) datatype- datatype of each receive buffer element (handle) source - rank of source (integer) tag - message tag (integer) comm - communicator (handle)`
			Receive a message

6	MPI_Finalize	`MPI_Finalize(void)`	All processes execute to terminate MPI

Example 1:

1. Two worker nodes send Greeting messages to the server node
2. Server node receives Greeting message and prints on display

Partial code running on all nodes including the server for Example 1 is shown below:

```
...
MPI_Comm_rank(MPI_COMM_WORLD, &my_rank);
gherr = gethostname( hname, silen);
//function returns hostnameto Array hname

if (my_rank != 0) { // Worker code
sprintf(message, "Greetings from process %d on %s!", my_rank, hname);
   dest = 0;
   MPI_Send(message, strlen (message)+1, MPI_CHAR, dest,tag, MPI_COMM_WORLD);
 } else
{
// Server code
```

```
printf ("Messages received by process %d on %s.\n\n", my_rank, hname);
 for (source = 1; source < p; source++) {
    MPI_Recv(message, 800, MPI_CHAR, source, tag, MPI_COMM_WORLD, &status);
    printf("%s\n", message);
   }
```

Example 2:

This example mathematical expression shown below is computed on the Linux cluster containing one server and three worker machines.

F= (a-b) (a+b) (a*b)

The problem can be divided into four parts shown below:

Sub operation 1:   t1 = (a – b) (completed by Machine1)

Sub operation 2:   t2 = (a + b) (completed by Machine2)

Sub operation 3:   t3 = (a * b) completed by Machine3

 Sub operation 4: F=t1*t2*t2   (completed by Machine4 (Server))

Partial C code for Machine1:

```
MPI_Comm_rank(MPI_COMM_WORLD, &my_rank);
...
if(my_rank==1)
{//Receiving variable a and b from server
MPI_Recv (&a, 1, MPI_DOUBLE, 0, tag, MPI_COMM_WORLD, &status);
MPI_Recv (&b, 1, MPI_DOUBLE, 0, tag, MPI_COMM_WORLD, &status);

double t1=a-b;
int dest=0        // ID for server

// Sending partial result to t1 to server
// node

MPI_Send(&t1, 1, MPI_DOUBLE, dest, tag, MPI_COMM_WORLD);
}
```

Partial code for Machine2

```
MPI_Comm_rank(MPI_COMM_WORLD,&my_rank);
...
...
if(my_rank==2)
{
// Receiving variable a and b from server

MPI_Recv (&a, 1, MPI_DOUBLE, 0, tag, MPI_COMM_WORLD, &status);

MPI_Recv (&b, 1, MPI_DOUBLE, 0, tag,
          MPI_COMM_WORLD, &status);

double t2=a+b;
int dest=0        // ID for server
// Sending partial result to server node
MPI_Send(&t2, 1, MPI_DOUBLE, dest, tag,
                     MPI_COMM_WORLD);
}
```

```
Partial code for Machine 3:

MPI_Comm_rank(MPI_COMM_WORLD, &my_rank);
...
...if(my_rank==3)
{
// Receiving variable a and b from server
MPI_Recv (&a, 1, MPI_DOUBLE, 0, tag,
            MPI_COMM_WORLD, &status);
MPI_Recv (&b, 1, MPI_DOUBLE, 0, tag,
            MPI_COMM_WORLD, &status);

double t3=a*b;
int dest=0        // ID for server

// Sending t3 to server node
MPI_Send(&t3, 1, MPI_DOUBLE, dest, tag,
                    MPI_COMM_WORLD);
}
```

```
Partial code for Server node

MPI_Comm_rank(MPI_COMM_WORLD, &my_rank);
if(my_rank==0) //server code.
{
// Server reads variables and send to three nodes.
printf("Please enter variables a and b");
scanf("%lf%lf", &a,&b);
//sending variable a and b to nodes 1 & 2
MPI_Send(&a, 1, MPI_DOUBLE, 1, tag,
                    MPI_COMM_WORLD);
MPI_Send(&b, 1, MPI_DOUBLE,  1, tag,
                    MPI_COMM_WORLD);
MPI_Send(&a, 1, MPI_DOUBLE, 2, tag,
                    MPI_COMM_WORLD);
MPI_Send(&b, 1, MPI_DOUBLE,  3, tag,
                    MPI_COMM_WORLD);
// Server receives partial results from nodes

MPI_Recv(&t1, 1, MPI_DOUBLE, 1, tag,
            MPI_COMM_WORLD, &status);
MPI_Recv (&t2, 1, MPI_DOUBLE, 2, tag,
            MPI_COMM_WORLD, &status);
MPI_Recv (&t3, 1, MPI_DOUBLE, 3, tag,
            MPI_COMM_WORLD, &status);

// Server computes final result
    f=t1*t2*t3;
    printf("The output is f=%lf",f);}
```

Example 3:

This example shows matrix multiplication on PC Cluster. For the sake of simplicity we consider the case of multiplication of 4X4 matrix with a 4x1 matrix. Total 5 nodes (server+4 slave nodes) will be required for matrix multiplication. The product matrix will consist of 4 rows and one column. Four elements of the product matrix will be generated by 4 slave nodes. Complete C code for this matrix example is given below:

```
#include<stdio.h>
#include"mpi.h"
int  main(int argc,char** argv)
{
int   myrank,
nprocs, n, i, islave, master, count;
MPI_Status   status;
Int      ierr,
resultlen, tag;
char hostname[MPI_MAX_PROCESSOR_NAME];
double     t0, t1, t2;
tag = 50;
int s;

/* Initialize MPI
 */
MPI_Init(&argc, &argv);

/* Get my rank id and number of MPI processes
*/
MPI_Comm_rank(MPI_COMM_WORLD, &myrank);
MPI_Comm_size(MPI_COMM_WORLD, &nprocs);

// matrix initialization
int a[4][4]={ 1,1,2,3 ,
        2,3,4,1 ,
        3,4,5,1 ,
        3,2,3,4  };
int b[4]={1,2,3,5};

int
a1[4],a2[4],a3[4],a4[4];
int j;

if ( myrank == 0 )
{
//----------------- Master part --------------------
/* Master will receive product matrix elements from  slaves  in integer r */
int r,k;
for(i=1;i<nprocs;i++)

{
MPI_Recv(&r,1, MPI_INT, i, tag,
MPI_COMM_WORLD,&status);
printf("%d\n ",r);
}
        }
/ Each slave part computes each element of the product matrix  and send to the master node*/
else
{
master = 0;
int s=0;
for(i=0;i<4;i++)
s=s+a[myrank-1][i]*b[i];
MPI_Send(&s,1,
MPI_INT,0,tag,MPI_COMM_WORLD);
}
MPI_Finalize();
}
```

In the matrix multiplication example, server node does not need to send multiplicand matrices to the slave nodes because each slave gets copies of both matrices.

All above codes are running in parallel on four nodes inside the cluster. Server node reads the variable and distribute to three nodes using MPI_Send function. Each worker machine receives variables from server node by using MPI_Recv function. Each computes its portion of computation and returns partial result to the server using MPI_Send function. Server collects partial results from worker nodes using MPI_Recv function, computes the final result and prints it. User will see inputs variables on the server node. Program output will be printed on the server node's console.

REMOTE ACCESS OF CLUSTER FOR PARALLEL PROCESSING

As it has been shown in section IV, before parallel jobs could be started, a parallel programming environment (PPE) is launched on all participating node. To initiate PPE, a non root user logs on the NFS/NIS server node or "head node" and issues the necessary commands. Once PPE is running the parallel code is executed by issuing "mpirun" command specifying the number of nodes one which the parallel job is to be run. Therefore, for cluster's remote access, only the head node S1 is made accessible to the remote sites as shown in Figure 4. Head node will have a TCP/IP connectivity to the LAN connecting all cluster nodes and to the UOH Intranet. UOH's Intranet is accessible by Internet by Virtual Private Network (VPN) set up on Internet client machines. The VPN configuration on Internet client machines will allow users to access the Linux cluster seamlessly.

Once a user is connected to UOH Intranet, he or she can access the LINUX cluster by one of the following ways:
1. Telnet: Telnet is a terminal emulator program running in text mode. On Windows or Linux machines users type telnet < hostname >, where hostname is host name of UOH cluster's head node or an ip address.
2. ssh PuTTY: This is similar to telnet but it is a secure shell. To connect to cluster,
  i. Run putty.exe
  ii. Choose SSH protocol
  iii. Enter the UOH cluster's head nodes' hostname, or IP address
  iv. Enter username and password
3. VNC[8]: Virtual Network Computing is useful if one needs to run graphics applications and can view graphical desktop from anywhere on the Internet. To run VNC,
i. Connect to head node using telnet or ssh.
ii. Make sure /usr/X11R6/bin is the PATH environment variable.
iii. Start a vncserver process. On head node by running /usr/bin/vncserver command.
iv. First time vncserver is run set up a password. This password is for making a connection to vncserver process and can be different from your login password. Run vncserver again once the password is set.
v. Run the vncviewer program on your PC. Enter the given display name and then enter the password for vncserver. VNC will bring the graphical desktop environment of the remote machine on your PC.

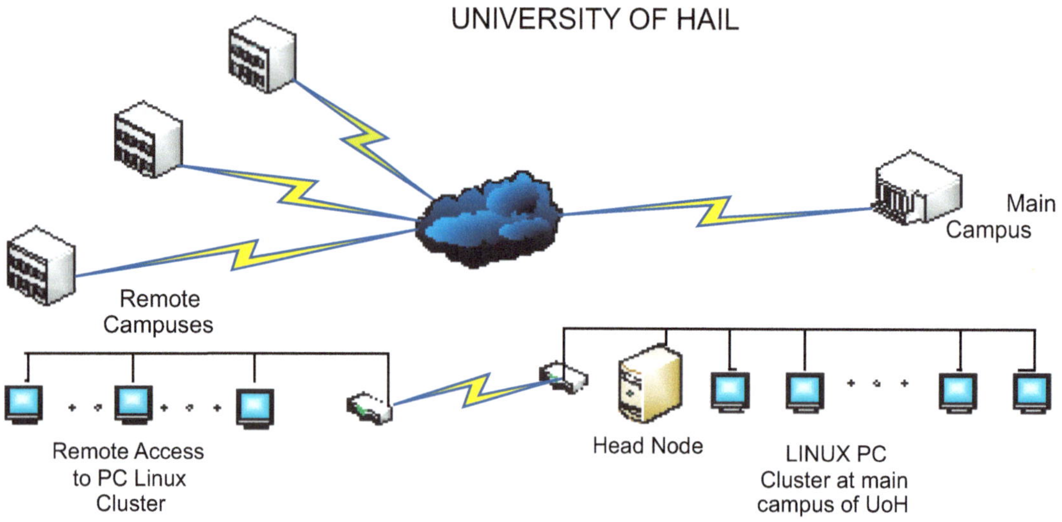

UNIVERSITY OF HAIL

Fig. 4. Remote users can access the head node of LINUX PC Cluster at Main Bldg via internet.

To disconnect, just close the VNC client window on your PC. There is no need to log out from the remote machine. When you reconnect to your vncserver sometime later, the desktop environment will be the same as when you left it. To stop vncserver on remote machine run the command: vncserver –kill <display name>, e.g. vncserver –kill S1:1, where S1 is head node.

SUMMARY

Parallel computing is used for achieving fast computational results in variety of areas ranging from engineering applications to commercial applications. An economical solution for structuring parallel computing system is possible by connecting customary Intel based PCs by a network. This ensemble of PCs can form a cluster of workstations. By using Message Passing Interface MPI, this cluster can be used for implementing parallel algorithms. This paper has discussed the details of building a PC cluster. We have discussed some simple example parallel programs to motivate users to utilize the PC cluster. Also remote access to the cluster further makes it cost effective solution of parallel computing solution for geographically dispersed users' community. Access of the cluster for parallel processing may be extended kingdom wide scientific community.

ACKNOWLEDGEMENT

Authors would like to acknowledge the University of Hail for providing the research infrastructure to complete this research proposal. Special acknowledgements are due to Mr. Razaat Chishty and Mr. Muhammad Saleem, of Information Technology Center (ITC), University of Hail, for their support in extending the Linux cluster to University's Intranet and to the Internet via VPN.

APPENDIX: STEPS FOR BUILDING A LINUX CLUSTER

This appendix explains complete steps of building a 3 nodes PC cluster. These steps can be used to construct a cluster of any size.

1.   INSTALLATION OF LINUX ENTERPRISE EDITION AND CONFIGURATION OF PC'S

Building Pentium cluster requires installation of Linux operating system on each node in the cluster. There are several flavors of Linux operating systems are available. We use RED Hat Linux Enterprise edition was installed on all Pentium machines [9].   The process begins by inserting first CD of Linux Enterprise edition on each PC. The installation process will be completed by following the installation instructions. During the installation process, node names should be assigned as well. S1 will be server and S2 and S3 will be nodes respectively.

POST INSTALLATION CONFIGURATIONS

1.1. NETWORK SERVER AND LAM CONFIGURATIONS.

After installation is complete, some applications must be installed on Network server such as LAM (Local Area Multicomputer environment).
Logon on each PC respectively and launch package management utility (Application □ System setting Add/Remove Applications).
In Package Management window, go to "Servers" section, check mark "Network Servers and Legacy Network Servers"
For Legacy server, click "details" on right hand side and check mark "rsh-servers" in the details window.
For Network servers, click "details" on the right hand side and check mark, "ypservers" in the details window (do this on server node only)
In Package Management window, go to "Applications" section and check mark "Engineering and Scientific" check box. Click "details" on right hand side and check mark "lam- The LAM programming environment.
Click "update in Package Management window, and follow the update instructions. This will require various Linux Enterprise CDs.

1.2. TCP/IP CONFIGURATION.

In order to assign IP addresses to each node in the network, the Network Interface Card (NIC) should be mapped with IP address and activated. To do this logon on each PC as root and start network device control tool by choosing Application → System Tools → Network Device Control. In Network Device Control window, click "Configure" button on right hand side. Click "Edit" button in Network configuration window and manually assign IP address and network mask. Then click "Activate" button in Network configuration window.

2. NETWORK SETTING

Once network is setup, connect each machine to an Ethernet switch and verify network connectivity to each PC by using ping command (Syntax: $ping <IP address>.)
On each PC log on as root and complete the network configuration by the following steps:
1. Edit /etc/hosts file and enter a list of IP addresses and their corresponding host- names:
    127.0.0.1 localhost.localdomain   localhost
    198.168.255.1   S1   s1

198.168.255.n   Sn sn < n is the client ID >

2. Edit /etc/host.conf file to specify the order of queries to resolve host name:
   order hosts, bind
   multi on

Host-specific Configuration Files

1. Edit /etc/HOSTNAME file to specify system hostname. This file should contain   the machine names such as (s1, s2, s3,…, s17)

2. Edit /etc/sysconfig/network file to specify a gateway host, gateway device:
   NETWORKING=yes
   HOSTNAME=<machinename>
   GATEWAYDEV=eth0
   NISDOMAIN=cluster

3. Edit /etc/sysconfig/network-scripts/ifcfg-eth0 file to have information needed to activate the network:

DEVICE=eth0
BOOTPROTO=none
ONBOOT=yes
IPADDR = <host IP address>
NETMASK=255.255.255.0
NETWORK=198.168.255.0
BROADCAST=198.168.255.255
USERCTL=no
PEERDNS=no
TYPE=ethernet

3. SERVER SETUP

This step will configure S1 as NFS and NIS server.

1. Check the network part is setup by pinging each machine.

2. Next set up the daemons to ensure they automatically start at boot-up.
   • Type setup
   • Highlight System Services
   • Press the Enter key
   • Make sure that only the following daemons are activated (Press Space to select or deselect): anacron, apmd, atd, autofs, crond, gpm, ipchains, iptables, keytable, lpd, netfs, network, nfs, nfslock, pcmcia, portmap, random, rawdevices, rlogin, rsh, rwalld, sshd, syslog, xfs, xinetd, ypbind, yppasswdd, ypserv
   • Press Tab, Tab and click Quit

3.1 NFS SERVER

NFS (Network File System) is a distributed file system which allows users of one system to access the files on another system as they were mounted on the local machines. This file sharing is over TCP/IP network. The machine which exports the file system is called NFS server and the machines mounting the remote file system are called NFS nodes.

1. Edit /etc/exports file to specify the files systems to be shared, hosts to be allowed to access the file systems and the type of permissions. Ensure you enter the following entries in file:

   /home s2 (rw,sync)
   /home s3 (rw,sync)
   /usr/export s2(rw,sync)
   /usr/export s2(rw,sync)

2. Create the directory /usr/export
      $> mkdir /usr/export

3. Enter the following command so the NFS daemons check this file for new information:
      $> /usr/sbin/exportfs -a

4. Reboot the computer
      $> shutdown -r now

5. Login again as root, then check if NFS works:
      $> rpcinfo -p

Check if mountd and nfs daemons are present.

3.2 NIS SERVER

NIS (Network Information System) formerly known as yellow pages, is an extension of NFS used to distribute system information between networked hosts. NIS is a distributed database system, which simply allows to maintain common configuration files such as /etc/hosts, /etc/passwd, /etc/group, etc) at one place. Machines using NIS can retrieve these files from NIS server as needed. Simply, NIS allows users to log on from anywhere in a NIS domain. NIS information is propagated to the NIS nodes

1. Set up the NIS domain by entering:
   $> nisdomainname cluster

2. Edit /etc/sysconfig/network file to add a domain name, e.g. cluster, by inserting:
   NISDOMAIN= cluster

3. Edit the /etc/yp.conf file by specifying the NIS server (S1):
   ypserver s1
   domain cluster server s1

4. Start up the ypserv daemon from /etc/rc.d/init.d:
   $> /etc/rc.d/init.d/ypserv restart

5. Edit the /etc/nsswitch.conf file and ensure that you have the following entries:
    passwd: files nis nisplus
    group: files nis nisplus
    hosts: files nis nisplus dns

Note: The order is important. The server machine will look for the password and hosts information first in its local files, and if it cannot find it there, searches it via the Network Information System.
Add a # before the line beginning with shadow.

6. Create the NIS (YP) database by running:

   $>/usr/lib/yp/ypinit -m

A line will appear

next host to add:

S1 is already listed as the server, so just press Control - D. Then type in y and press Enter.

If you need to update a map later, run make in the /var/yp directory, once you add a new user.

7. Run make:

$> cd /var/yp

$> make

8. Restart the ypbind daemon:

$>/etc/rc.d/init.d/ypbind restart

9. Create a new user with the name ypuser and password XXXX

$> useradd ypuser

$> passwd ypuser

Set the password and confirm it.

10. Update the map by running make in the /var/yp directory. Do this every time you add a new user.

$> cd /var/yp

$> make

11. Make sure that the NIS knows about ypuser

$> ypcat passwd

12. Edit the /etc/hosts.equiv file. Make sure that you have the following entries:

S1+

S2

S3

4. CLIENT SETUP

Our client setups are performed on s2 and s3. First reboot the machine and then login as a root user.

4.1 NETWORK CHECK

1. Make sure the ethernet card is set up right. Try to ping yourself and the server. To stop ping, press Ctrl - C

$> ping s1

2. Next set up the daemons to ensure they automatically start at boot-up.

• Type setup

• Highlight System Services

• Press the Enter key

• Make sure that only the following daemons are activated (press Space to select or deselect): anacron, apmd, atd, autofs, crond, gpm, ipchains, iptables, keytable, lpd, netfs, network, nfslock, pcmcia, portmap, random, rawdevices, rlogin, rsh, sshd, syslog, xfs, xinetd, ypbind

• Press Tab, Tab and click Quit

3. Since rsh is needed set it up manually:

• In a terminal go to /etc/xinetd.d

$> cd /etc/xinetd.d

• Edit rsh and change the entry disabled from yes to no.

• Restart the xinetd daemon:

$> /etc/rc.d/init.d/xinetd restart
4. Test rsh by typing:
  $> rsh S1
When it asks for the password, interrupt rsh by pressing Ctrl-D.
Network should be working now.

4.2 NFS CLIENT

Now set up the client to share a filesystem from our server S1. On each NFS client do the following:
1. Run /etc/rc.d/init.d/portmap restart. To start the portmap daemon:
  $> /etc/rc.d/init.d/portmap restart
2. For this cluster S1 will be a server that allows you to mount the file systems and use its resources. Make a new directory on your client machine:
  $> mkdir /usr/export
3. Mount the directory /usr/export from S1 onto the /usr/export directory of your local host.
  $> mount –t nfs s1:/usr/export/usr/export
  $> df (check if /usr/export is there)
4. Check that /usr/export   reflects the content of /usr/export directory on S1:
  $> cd /usr/export
  $> ls
  $> cd
  $> umount /usr/export (this will unmount the /usr/export directory)
  $> df
5. Next mount the /home directory from S1:
  $> umount /home
  $> mount -t nfs S1:/home   /home
6. Edit /etc/fstab file to automate the mount process. This step will allow mounting the /usr/export and /home every time the machine starts. The entry in the /etc/fstab file may look as follows:

  s1:/usr/export /usr/export nfs   user,   exec, dev, suid, rw, defaults   0 0
  S1:/home /home nfs   user, exec, dev, suid, rw, defaults 0 0

7. Reboot the machine (shutdown -r now) and make sure that S1:/user/export and /home are mounted.

4.3 NIS CLIENT

To setup the NIS clients, following steps are needed for each NIS client machine.
1. Set up the NIS domain by entering:
   $> nisdomainname cluster
2. Edit the /etc/yp.conf file by specifying the NIS server:
   ypserver s1
   domain cluster server s1
4. Edit the /etc/passwd file. Make sure that you have the following entry in bottom line:

+::::::
5. Edit the /etc/nsswitch.conf file and ensure that you have the following entries:
   passwd: nis files nisplus
   group: nis files nisplus
   hosts: files nis nisplus dns
   Add a # before the line begin with shadow.
6. Use setup to ensure all the daemons needed, will start automatically at boot time.
   • In the terminal type in command setup.
   • Select System Services
   • Press the Enter key
   • Select the following daemon with space key:
ypbind
   • Using the Tab key to get OK and then exit.
   • Reboot the computer
   • Restart ypbind using the command line
      $>/etc/rc.d/init.d/ypbind restart
7. Edit the /etc/hosts.equiv file. Make sure that you have the following entries:
   S1 +
8. Reboot NIS client login as ypuser. Use the password you defined in the server setup.

5. CONFIGURATION OF PASSWORD LESS SECURE SHELL (SSH)

In order to launch LAM environment on each node of the cluster, we need to configure password-less SSH so that we don't need to provide password for each cluster node. For this purpose, log on to server or master node and run following series of commands:

$ mkdir ~/.ssh
$ chmod 700 ~/.ssh
$ cd ~/.ssh
$ ssh-keygen -t rsa
$ scp ~/.ssh/id_rsa.pub <login>@<hostname >:<working$directory>/id_rsa_remote.pub
$ssh<login>@<hostname>(enter password)
$cat id_rsa_remote.pub >> .ssh/ authorized_ keys
$chmod 644 .ssh/authorized_keys
In the above commands, hostname is the name of machine which you want to log on without entering user password. The working directory above is /home/username.
Running MPI program:
You can now run the program using the command mpirun as shown below:
$mpirun -np 3 hello
The option -np specifies how many processors you want to run your program on. So in this case, 3 processes will be invoked on three different nodes. When finished running your LAM-MPI jobs, you need to shut down the communications daemons. You do this with the following command:
$lamhalt -v machinefile

6. CLUSTER UPGRADING

Sometime it is required a cluster node becomes faulty or needs to be replaced by a more powerful nodes. In a LINUX Cluster, in order to use public-key secure connection with other hosts (ssh, scp, sftp) there is a special directory, ~/.ssh/, where passphrases and public keys are stored. In ~/.ssh/ directory, a file called *known_hosts* contains information about the cluster nodes ever contributed in lam Parallel Programming environment. If a node has been replaced by another new node, then it will get new MAC address. As *known_hosts* file will retain the finger prints of old node, the entry of the previous node should be removed from *known_hosts.* to include new node in the cluster

REFERENCES

[1]   Anderson, T.E., D.E. Culler and Peterson, "A case of NOW (Cluster of workstations", IEEE Micro Vol. 15, No.1, pp. 54-64.

[2]   Syed Misbahuddin and Fazal Noor, "Hands-on Workshop on Parallel Processing", Department of Computer Science and Software engineering, University of Hail, Saudi Arabia, May 2007.

[3]   Chandra R., L. Dagum D. Kohr. D. Maydan, J. McDonald and R. Menon " Parallel Programming in OpenMP", Margon Kaufmann Publishers, San Francisco, CA, 2001

[4]   Pacheco P. "Parallel Programming with MPI", Morgan Kaufmann Publishers San Francisco, CA, 1997

[5]   http://www.mcs.anl.gov/mpi/mpich/

[6]   http://www.lam-mpi.org/

[7]   Edinburgh Parallel Computing Centre, University of Edinburgh. CHIMP Concepts, June 1991.

[8]   www.realvnc.com

[9]   www.redhat.com

CHAPTER 3

High Performance Linux Clusters For Breaking RSA

Athar Mahboob (1), Nassar Ikram (1) and Junaid Zubairi (2)

(1) National University of Sciences & Technology, Pakistan
(2) State University of New York at Fredonia, USA
athar@penc.edu.pk, nassar@nust.edu.pk, zubairi@cs.fredonia.edu

Abstract: High performance compute clusters have been used in recent years to tackle hard problems in the domain of cryptography and breaking many encryption algorithms. Integer factorization is a hard mathematical problem which forms the basis of many public key cryptographic schemes such as the RSA algorithm. To date the largest integer factored is about 200 digits long. This factorization was made possible by use of distributed computing and use of clusters. We present results of our work on setting up single server image clusters using Kerrighed Single System Image based cluster. We have attempted to use a number of factoring algorithms and their well-known implementations. Our clustering recipes and results shall be useful to others who are planning to setup Linux clusters for high-performance computing.

In this contribution we also provide the current state of open source Linux based clustering solutions. A challenging reality is that many open source clustering projects are simply dying a slow or fast death. These include OpenMosix and even OpenSSI. Other open source clustering projects too have been very slow with releases. Open source clustering software projects exhibit paradoxical trends. Commercial software was donated by a vendor as a seed for open source cluster software community (HP/Compaq TruClusters as a seed for OpenSSI). Mosix on the other hand went from open source software project to commercial product after its initial success on Linux platform. Very recently the open source community of Mosix (completely distinct from the Mosix product) functioning as OpenMosix for several years has now declared the project going to be defunct soon citing the appearance of multiple core CPUs as one major reason for it. In this contribution we hope to identify the promising high performance clustering toolkit for the next few years to come.

INTRODUCTION

Scalability and availability through clusters of computers is a paradigm that has received more than three decades of attention. Drastically reduced hardware prices, development of commodity high speed local area network communication and increased reliability of hardware components motivated the development of low priced clusters that offered throughput matching that of expensive supercomputers. The advances in hardware were matched in the software arena by the development of general purpose operating systems and high level languages with a plethora of software libraries. Linux operating system revolutionized the software landscape and provided the much needed open source kernel to run open source software on broad variety of hardware platforms. Many clustering solutions have been developed for Linux. Even without any specialized software, Linux computers on a network can form a cluster to collaborate with each other using remote shell execution and shared directories. Use of portable code with well defined standards leads to increasingly efficient use of clusters [Bader 2001] because users do not have to redesign applications while migrating to better clusters. MPI [MPI Forum 2008] and PVM [PVM 1997] are such standard parallel programming interfaces that use message passing mechanism. PVM was developed at Oak Ridge National Laboratory in 1989 as part of a distributed computing research project whereas MPI was specified by a committee of industry and research experts in 1993 and implemented in Argonne National Laboratory. MPI is more suitable to data parallel problems whereas both standards provide message passing libraries for development of portable parallel applications [Gropp 2002]. MPI has been implemented and released as MPICH

[MPICH2 2009] using 'Chameleon' as the portability layer and LAM [LAM/MPI 2008], originally released by Ohio Supercomputing center. LAM is now replaced by Open MPI [OpenMPI 2009], a project of academics and industry to implement MPI-2 library for achieving high performance computing. As of July 2009, its latest version was v1.3.3.

Two broad applications of clusters are in the business and scientific domain. Business users have primarily required clusters which can handle a variety of computational load of similar nature. The computational load consists of business transactions where each transaction may be of moderate complexity but a large number of such transactions have to be processed per unit time. On the other hand, problems in scientific research require computational capability to solve a single simulation or calculation which may be of high complexity. The problem is then broken in smaller problems and the smaller problems are distributed among a number of computational nodes for concurrent processing.

The users require the clusters to be highly available and scalable to adapt to various sizes of problems. Availability is primarily driven by business uses of computers where down-time due to failures or preventive maintenance cannot be tolerated as it may result in loss of revenue. Availability in clusters is achieved with automatic fail-over techniques in case a node fails so that the healthy nodes continue to function normally. Scalability has a few aspects including computational scalability and network communication scalability. A highly scalable cluster would increase in size to include more systems in response to increasing computational load. OSCAR [OSCAR 2009] is a Beowulf clustering tool that establishes highly scalable Linux clusters in which nodes can leave or join the cluster during its normal operation. OSCAR deals with diverse *nix environments and provides flexible and easy to use package that can be used to configure and program the cluster. HA-OSC AR [HA-OSCAR 2003] achieves high availability through redundancy of components. It establishes a self-healing mechanism that includes failure detection and recovery actions, automatic fail-over and fail-back techniques. It uses redundant master nodes, recovery from disk crashes and cluster-wide security.

SSI (Single System Image) clusters target the presentation of the cluster as one big machine with seamless integration of resources and applications. Some SSI projects include Kerrighed [Kerrighed 2004], and OpenSSI [OpenSSI 2006]. The logical architecture of a SSI cluster is shown in Figure 1inspired from the presentation in [OpenSSI 2006]. Kerrighed offers the view of a single SMP (Symmetric Multiprocessing) system on top of a cluster and allows a global process scheduler that can be dynamically configured. OpenSSI system configures processes with unique PID's across the cluster and achieves process and filesystem SSI. The distributed memory is merged into a virtual shared memory presenting the view of a tightly coupled system. Kerrighed can perform task balancing with the scheduler by allowing the migration of tasks from overloaded nodes to underloaded nodes. OpenSSI contains similar capability known as 'leveling' where processes can be migrated to level off the loads.

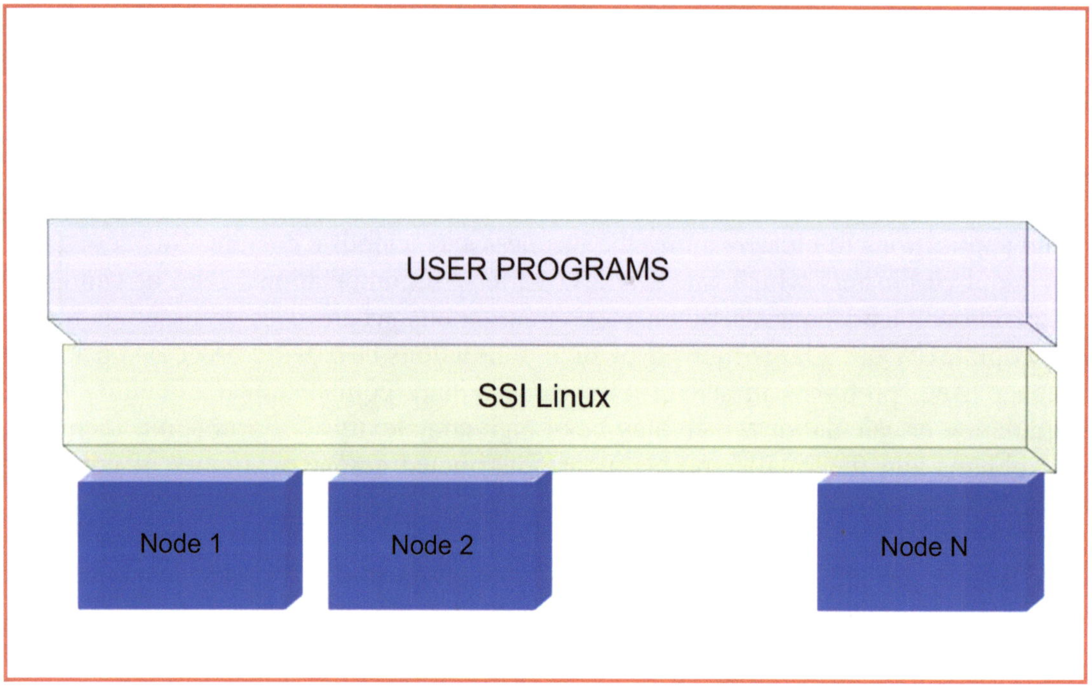

Fig. 1. Logical Architecture of Single System Image Linux Cluster

LINUX OPERATING SYSTEM AND ITS EVOLUTION

Even though open source and free software has a long and colorful history but Linux operating system stands out as its most significant expression. Linux is a fresh implementation of the UNIX operating system design philosophy. Main features of this philosophy are simplicity, modularity, portability, well defined interfaces and flexibility [Raymond 2003]. Linux embodies these design principles.

Like its predecessors, the BSD UNIX, Linux has become the testbed of new ideas in operating systems research. Clustering has been extensively implemented on Linux. It is not possible here to enumerate each and every clustering project that has been tried on Linux so we shall be selective in our presentation. As a proof of Linux clustering capabilities, among the top 500 computers Linux based clusters occupy more than 85% of the slots [Top500a] as shown in figure 2.

As the cost of maintaining and developing operating systems software has become economically infeasible many commercial operating systems, like the Sun Solaris, have decided to go open source. Many others have contributed their key source code to Linux. One such example is the contribution by Silicon Graphics of its massively parallel processing code to Linux kernel. The operating system landscape has seen many changes in the last two decades. The rise of Linux as the pre-eminent and dominant Unix type of operating system is one such change.

It is amazing that Linux has not run out of steam despite its age. The Linux kernel development community is strong and active. New features are being added into the Linux Kernel at a very fast pace. All facets of the Linux operating system kernel have been developing steadily. Despite such a vigorous development in the Linux Kernel components clustering is not yet a part of the mainstream kernel. One of the reasons for this is the development of multi-core CPUs and the mature support for Symmetrical Multiprocessing (SMP) in the Linux Kernel. Many users have found that the performance offered by SMP computers meets their computational requirements. It can therefore be concluded that clustering has been left as an exercise for the end user. It is treated as a customization. There are valid reasons to do so. One clustering approach simply does not fit all requirements.

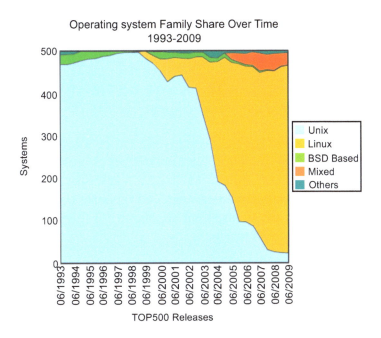

Fig. 2. Historical Trend of Operating System Share Among Top 500 Super Computers

TYPES OF CLUSTERS

Clusters are of various types. Each type of cluster provides either scalability of some type or increases availability. Here we differentiate between single image clusters and other forms of clustering techniques such as Linux Virtual Server Load Balancer, Beowulf Compute Cluster, Linux High Availability Clusters, and Single Server Image Clusters such as Mosix, OpenSSI and Kerrighed. Following are the types of clusters:

1. Compute Clusters
2. Load Balancing Clusters
3. Storage Clusters
4. Single Server Image Clusters

Compute Cluster

A compute cluster provides us with scalability of computational power. There are two basic approaches for a compute cluster. In the first approach each node in a compute cluster runs a separate instance of operating system and has its own process and memory space. The nodes cooperate and share computational load by means of a high-level message passing application programming interface such as the PVM or MPI. In this approach each node maintains its distinct identity and the may even be running different operating systems.

Load Balancing Cluster

In a load balancing cluster a front-end node receives the original request from the clients and then relays the request to one of an array of back-end servers. This way the incomings requests are distributed and shared among a number of servers according to some policy. The policy may be round-robin or each node may be assigned a weight. In some situations the weight values may be dynamically adjusted based on the load feed back received from the nodes. The front end node bears the burden of communication with the clients whereas the back-end nodes bear the burden of processing each request and accessing and/or updating of any persistent information stored in a database. One of the benefits of this load balancing cluster technique is that the front-end node may maintain a heart-beat with each of the back-end nodes to determine node health. Then, if any of the back-end nodes fail, they shall not be sent any further requests. Thus this arrangement increases the availability by keeping the node failures hidden from the end users.

The best example of the load balancing cluster is the Linux Virtual Server (LVS) project. In LVS the front-end node is called the Director. The Director unfortunately can become a single point of failure itself, thus decreasing availability. The solution is to use redundant Director nodes where the Director and its standby maintain a heartbeat and replicate connection information so that the failure of the Director is totally transparent to clients. A typical LVS cluster topology with redundant Director nodes is shown in Figure 3.

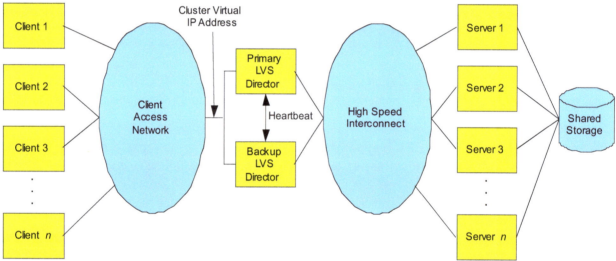

Fig. 3. Typical LVS Load Balancing Cluster Topology

Storage Cluster

The objective of a storage cluster is to increases the size, speed and availability of the data storage system. At the basic level RAID technology is a storage cluster. At the next level come the Storage Area Network (SAN) technology. Storage clustering technology is mature. Linux has economical forms of storage cluster available in the form of Distributed Replicated Block Device (DRBD). The storage cluster forms one component of a high performance computer system and is used to scale performance and ensure that the storage subsystem of the computer system does not become the performance bottleneck.

Single Server Image Cluster

The Single Server Image (SSI) clustering technique tries to combine the various types of clustering into one elegant clustering solution. In SSI clustering a virtual bigger SMP system is created out of the cluster nodes. This type of clustering in fact tries to make clustering transparent to applications. Processes can be seamlessly migrated without the need for using any specific programming API. The memory space and the process space of the entire cluster is unified. Standard software tools can be used to monitor the system as if it was just a SMP node.

LIMITATIONS OF CLUSTERS

Despite all the hype surrounding clusters there are some limitations to performance offered by clusters. If a single computer takes 'x' amount of time to run a computation, two computers would ideally take 'x/2' time to run the same computation. However, practical speedup is never 100% and in fact in some situations, adding a new computer may even hurt instead of helping accelerate the computation. To see why we cannot achieve ideal speedup with clusters, consider the following issues:

∞ There is considerable overhead in parallelizing a program. Parallelizing would involve segmenting out the code sections that can be run in parallel and transferring the code segments and the data required to the selected computer. We also need to synchronize various nodes of the cluster and collect and integrate the results that are returned by the nodes. Thus, the segmenting, communication and result integration overhead would clock extra time that was not needed in the single computer case.

∞ Any unresolved data dependencies, resource conflicts and I/O dependencies in the instructions would result in serial execution of the target instructions. Thus some part of the program would always be executed in serial even if we have enough computers in the cluster to parallelize the whole program. Amdahl's law states that the minimum time needed to execute a program on parallel computers can never be lower than the time taken by the serial part of the program. This law sets the upper limit on speedup of a program on parallel computers.

∞ For a small program, the change in speed may be insignificant when it is migrated to a cluster. However, if the program involves millions of calculations in parallelizable code segments, a significant speedup is achieved when it is run on a cluster.

∞ If the program is being moved from a well known platform to a cluster of machines on which the programmers have little or no experience, the chances of failure increase significantly. Thus, the suitability of clusters is dependent upon the platform of team expertise and the learning curve for the migration.

∞ Even if all the other drawbacks are negligible, the workload imbalance can result in little or no speedup. If tasks can be dynamically migrated between the nodes that communicate via message passing, communication overhead would also increase.

From the above discussion, we can state that not all problems are suitable for solving on clusters. One should not move a small problem to a large cluster in hopes of significant speedup. Similarly, if the program is written in a way that most of its code is serial, there is little or no benefit in moving it to a parallel cluster. Instead of moving the mostly serial program to the cluster, the algorithm and the program should be rewritten to take advantage of parallel hardware.

Managing a cluster of multiple machines is more difficult and the cost of running a cluster is higher than managing and running a single computer.

SINGLE SERVER IMAGE CLUSTERS IN THE LINUX WORLD

The major charm of Single Server Image (SSI) clusters is that they provides an elegant view of the cluster as a single SMP machine. In reality this is very hard to achieve given the diversity of hardware and latencies of inter-node communication. Each node has a number of peripherals and the control of those peripherals is localized. The abstraction of those peripherals into a unified view is not a trivial problem. Due to these reasons, the problem of single server image clustering has not been solved in its entirety. Nevertheless, the evolution of SSI clusters in the Linux arena is summarized in this section. We now review the development of Mosix, OpenMosix, OpenSSI and Kerrighed.

Mosix

Mosix is a clustering project that pre-dates Linux and was developed for UNIX type of operating systems. MOSIX has been researched and developed since 1977 at The Hebrew University of Jerusalem by the research team of Prof. Amnon Barak. So far, ten major versions have been developed. The first version, called MOS, for Multicomputer OS, (1981-83) was based on Bell Lab's Seventh Edition Unix and ran on a cluster of PDP-11 computers. Later versions were based on Unix System V Release 2 (1987-89) and ran on a cluster of VAX and NS32332-based computers, followed by a BSD/OS-derived version (1991-93) for a cluster of 486/Pentium computers [MOSIX 2009] . Since 1999 MOSIX is tuned to Linux for x86 platforms. MOSIX makes frequent releases and is keeping pace with mainstream Linux kernel by releasing its versions based on current kernel releases. However, restrictive nature of its software licensing keeps its user base limited and keeps it out of open source category.

openMosix

openMosix was an attempt of the Linux MOSIX community to develop a community based version of MOSIX after MOSIX became proprietary software in late 2001. However openMosix remained stuck with Linux Kernel version 2.4 and could not adapt to the version 2.6. Eventually the maintainer of openMosix announced plans to end the openMosix project effective March 1, 2008, claiming that "the increasing power and availability of low cost multi-core processors is rapidly making single-system image (SSI) clustering less of a factor in computing." Due to this reason openMosix is of historical interest only. The openMosix website main page shown in figure 4 summarizes the openMosix situation very well [OpenMosix 2009].

OpenSSI

OpenSSI has been an ambitious Linux clustering project [OpenSSI 2009]. The aim of the project was to avoid re-inventing the wheel and combine existing Linux clustering related projects in such a way so as to create the SSI cluster. Unfortunately the project has run out of steam. After a few years of active work only a few contributors remain committed to the project. Originally the project had a strong commitment and support from Hewlett-Packard. The last major release was made in 2006.

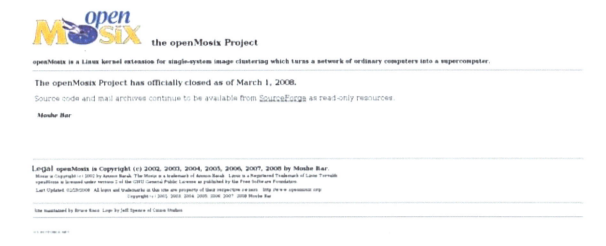

Fig, 4. openMosix Website Main Page

Kerrighed

The Kerrighed project was launched at the French National Research Laboratory (INRIA) in 1998. The project has thus been in existence for over a decade and may be regarded as mature. The project is still releasing newer version and adding features with every release. The current release is called Kerrighed 2 series. The Kerrighed 1 series had many more features but was not a stable platform. The Kerrighed 2 series removed many of the experimental features and is slowly adding back features as they are stabilized [Kerrighed 2009]. Admittedly the Kerrighed user community is also small.

THE CLUSTER BUILDING BLOCKS

Now we review the hardware and software required for cluster in a generic fashion. We discuss the master or boot server node, the cluster interconnect, the cluster compute or member nodes, the cluster operating system software, the middleware libraries such as Kerrighed libraries, etc. In figure 5 we show the generic view of the cluster nodes, the interconnect and the cluster boot server.

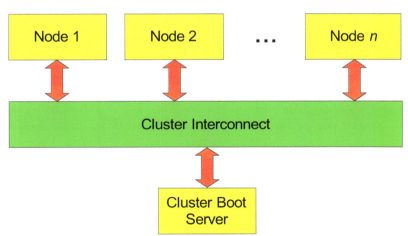

Fig. 5. Generic View of Cluster Components

Cluster Nodes

The cluster node itself is made up of a number of components. These components are shown in the figure below. The hardware components consist of the network interface, the system bus within the node through which all of the data moves while traveling from its CPU and memory to the network and so on. The node CPU is in control of the hardware resources of the node and runs an instance of the operating system supporting clustering. In the case of SSI clusters each node runs the same operating system image in every respect. The various components of the cluster node are shown in figure 6.

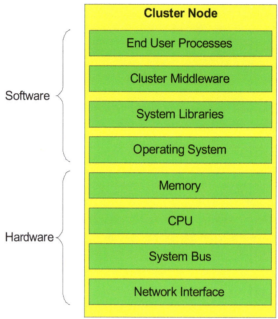

Fig. 6. Components of a cluster node

System libraries include the standard C and C++ libraries and any application libraries that may be needed. In SSI cluster the entire software stack is common to all nodes and is generally served as a network mounted root filesystem. In addition, libraries specific to cluster middle-ware may also be present.

Cluster Interconnect

The cluster nodes perform the inter-node communication using the interconnection network. One of the major limitation of the clustering technology is the speed and latency of the interconnection network. For those with limited budgets interconnection using Gigabit Ethernet is an appropriate choice. For the performance conscious clusters Infiniband is the technology of choice for cluster interconnect. Infiniband can give data throughputs reaching 100 Gbps with extremely low latencies.

As can be seen from figure 7, obtained from the Top500 data [Top500b] these two interconnection technologies dominate the high performance computer interconnect landscape. When looking at performance data we can see that even with Gigabit Ethernet interconnection network systems can perform well on performance benchmarks. This anomaly can be explained because the frequency and length of inter-node communication messages differs for various computational problems. This means that even with a low speed interconnection cluster systems running algorithms requiring fewer inter node messages will perform reasonably well.

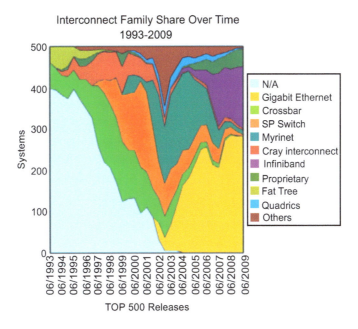

Fig. 7. Gigabit Ethernet and Infiniband Dominate Interconnection for HPC Clusters

The Cluster Boot Server

In order to allow the cluster nodes to easily load the required software we use the Cluster Boot Server as the solution. In this solution it is easy to add cluster nodes as no installation is required on the cluster nodes themselves. The cluster boot server itself is not part of the single server image cluster as its role is only to facilitate the cluster nodes in accessing and loading their software and configuration. For the sake of simplcity we can run the cluster boot server by using one of the standard modern Linux distributions such as Ubuntu, Suse or Redhat Linux. The essential components of the cluster boot server which require proper configuration are shown in the figure 8.

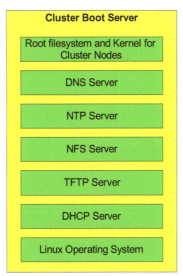

Fig. 8. Cluster Boot Server Components

The cluster boot server performs an important role by providing the infrastructure software to all cluster nodes. It ensures that identical operating system software and libraries are made available to cluster nodes. It also functions as the cluster management and configuration management component of the cluster.

KERRIGHED CLUSTER BUILDING PROCEDURE

In this section we explain our recipe of building a Kerrighed cluster. This is a recipe which is repeatable and provides solution to commonly faced problems as well. Furthermore, we also provide as a part of this recipe the procedure to virtualize parts of the cluster software as well as to effortlessly replicate/duplicate the clustering software as and when required. Our recipe started out with [EBC 2009] but has improved on many aspects and documented certain important steps which were missing in [EBC 2009]. We first provide a general description of the cluster node boot proecudre and then the specific commands to enable the installation ond proper configuration of the required services.

General Description of Cluster Node Boot Procedure

To make the cluster node operations fault free and plug & play the cluster node must be booted over the network. Most modern PC motherboards come ready with the capability to boot their operating system over the network using the technology called PXE (Pre-boot eXecution Environment) within the BIOS firmware. Once enabled through the BIOS settings menu the sequence of steps that takes place during the boot process is shown in the figure 9.

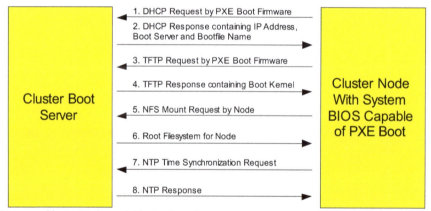

Fig. 9. Interaction Between Cluster Nodes and Cluster Boot Server

Once any cluster node boots it sends a Dynamic Host Configuration Protocol (DHCP) broadcast requesting TCP/IP configuration. The cluster boot server is running a properly configured instance of DHCP server service and responds with the following paramaters:

1. Node IP Address
2. Subnet Mask
3. Default Gateway
4. Domain Name
5. DNS Server
6. Boot Server
7. Boot Image Name

On getting the DHCP response the PXE firmware configures its IP address and then sends a Trivial File Transfer Protocol (TFTP) request to the Boot Server identified in the DHCP response. The TFTP request is made for the file Boot Image Name provided to the node. In general, the boot image can be different for each node. However, in our case since it is a Single System Image cluster therefore each node is provided with the same boot file. The boot file is infact a properly configured and compiled Linux kernel instance supporting all the required hardware and system capabilities requried by the cluster nodes. It should be noted that we need to record the Medium Access Control (MAC) address of Network Interface Card (NIC) of each cluster node before hand so that it can be assigned a deterministic TCP/IP configuration.

After the Linux kernel is booted the root filesystem is mounted over NFS. The Kernel boot parameters are configured as shown in the following example:

```
KERNEL vmlinuz-<KERNEL_VERSION>
APPEND root=/dev/nfs nfsroot=<BOOTSERVER_IP>:<NFS_ROOTFS_SHARE> ip=dhcp rw
```

It should be noted that a second DHCP configuration request is made by the same node, this time it is made by the TCP/IP networking stack in the Linux kernel. Once the root filesystem is mounted over NFS standard system initialization is done using the init scripts and the remaining services are properly started. These would include the Secure Shell server allowing us to remotely log on to any one of the cluster nodes to initiate jobs for the cluster. Another useful service would be the NTP client service. Each cluster node is able to synchronize its clock with that of the boot server using Network Time Protocol (NTP).

Specific Commands to Install Boot Server Components

Now we give the specific commands to enable the installation of Boot Server software components on Ubuntu Linux 9.04 distribution. Since a lot of Linux commands will be provided in the following material and sample text of configuration files will be provided our conventions should be noted:

1. Any line beginning with a $ character is a Linux command to be typed on a shell prompt.
2. Any text block beginning with a line # <some_file_name> # is a configuration file fragment provided as sample to be used to make appropriate changes to the file identified by <some_file_name>.

DHCP Server

The command to install the DHCP server package on Ubuntu Linux distribution is:

```
$ sudo aptitude install dhcp3-server
```

The use of sudo package to execute administrative commands is done as a system security measure. The super user account "root" is kept disabled by default in Ubuntu Linux. We preserve this behavior and use the sudo facility to execute administrative commands. To configure the DHCP server following steps are to be performed:

1. The file /etc/default/dhcp3-server contains the ethernet card to listen to DHCP requests. In our case it is eth0 so the file should read:

```
# /etc/default/dhcp3-server #
interfaces="eth0"
```

2. Next we edit /etc/dhcp3/dhcpd.conf so it looks like the following:

```
# /etc/dhcp3/dhcpd.conf #
# General options
option dhcp-max-message-size 2048;
use-host-decl-names on;
deny unknown-clients;
deny bootp;

# DNS settings
option domain-name "kerrighed";
option domain-name-servers 10.1.1.254;

# Information about the network setup
subnet 10.1.1.0 netmask 255.255.255.0 {
  option routers 10.1.1.254;
  option broadcast-address 10.1.1.255;  # Broadcast address for your network.
}

# Declaring IP addresses for nodes and PXE info

group {
  filename "pxelinux.0";              # location of PXE bootloader.
  option root-path "10.1.1.111:/nfsroot/kerrighed";  # Location of the bootable filesystem on NFS
server

  host kerrighednode1 {
      fixed-address 10.1.1.221;       # IP address for kerrighednode1.
      hardware ethernet 01:2D:61:AB:17:86; # MAC address of the kerrighednode1's ethernet
adapter
  }

  host kerrighednode2 {
      fixed-address 10.1.1.222;       # IP address for kerrighednode2.
      hardware ethernet 01:2D:61:AC:17:87; # MAC address of the kerrighednode2's ethernet
adapter
  }

... additional nodes ...

  server-name "bootserver"; # Name of the PXE server
  next-server 10.1.1.111;     # The IP address of the dhcp/tftp/nfs server
}
```

3. In order for configuration chages to take effect the dhcp server can be restarted by issuing the command

```
$ sudo /etc/init.d/dhcp3-server restart
```

4. In addition we would like the DHCP server to automatically start when the system is booted up. Following command makes the appropriate symbolic links in the System V type init setup:

```
$ sudo update-rc.d dhcp3-server defaults
```

Setting up the TFTP Server and PXE bootloader

The operating sytem boot image is served by the TFTP server. The TFTP server package can be installed by issuing the command:

```
$ sudo aptitude install tftpd-hpa
```

It is possible to run the TFTP server either directly or through the Inetd super server. For the cluster infrastructure it is best to run it directly. The configuration of the TFTP server is done as follows.

1. The settings for TFTP server are done by editing the file /etc/default/tftpd-hpa and making sure it looks like the following:

```
# /etc/default/tftp-hpa #
# Defaults for tftp-hpa
RUN_DAEMON="YES"
OPTIONS="-l -s /var/lib/tftpboot"
```

2. To enable network booting of clients we install syslinux bootloader and copy the PXE bootloader code to the tftp server directory.

```
$ sudo aptitude install syslinux
$ sudo cp /usr/lib/syslinux/pxelinux.0 /var/lib/tftpboot/
```

We create a directory to store the default configuration for all the nodes

```
$ sudo mkdir /var/lib/tftpboot/pxelinux.cfg
```

3. Create the file /var/lib/tftp/pxelinux.cfg/default and add the following default configuration for the nodes to boot:

```
LABEL linux
KERNEL vmlinuz-<KERNEL_VERSION>
APPEND root=/dev/nfs initrd=initrd.img-<KERNEL_VERSION> nfsroot=10.1.1.111:/nfsroot/kerrighed
ip=dhcp rw
```

4. Copy a standard Linux kernel to /var/lib/tftpboot/ in order to test the diskless-boot system. Replace <KERNEL_VERSION> with whatever you are using. For example, you could use the same Kernel that comes with the standard Ubuntu 9.04 installation that is being used on the boot server. This would assume that the cluster nodes support the same hardware archietcture that the boot server is using. The issue here is to ensure that if a 64-bit Linux kernel is being used on the boot server that cluster nodes should have a 64-bit processor to run the kernel. The case of 32 bit kernel does not cause any problems as 64 bit processors from Intel family can run both 32 bit and 64 bit versions of Linux.

```
$ sudo cp /boot/vmlinuz-<KERNEL_VERSION> /var/lib/tftpboot/
```

Alternatively the kernel version can be found by using the command:

```
$ uname -r
```

To enable the use of NFS based root file system it is necessary to change the initrd by performing the following steps:

5. Install the initramfs-tools by issuing the command:

$ aptitude install initramfs-tools

6. Configure initramfs-tools so that the initial ramdisk (initrd) is correctly built to support NFS mounted root filesystem. By default the initrd supports the use of lcoal devices (hard disks, USB, CD-ROM, etc.) for the root file system. Edit the file /etc/initramfs-tools/initramfs.conf:

```
# /etc/initramfs-tools/initramfs.conf #
#
# NFS Section of the config.
#

# BOOT: [ local | nfs ]
#
# local - Boot off of local media (harddrive, USB stick).

#
# nfs - Boot using an NFS drive as the root of the drive.
#
```

Change

BOOT=local

to

BOOT=nfs

7. Generate the new initrd by issuing the command

$ mkinitramfs -o /tmp/athar/initrd.img-`uname -r` -k

8. Finally, copy the initial ramdisk image to /boot

$ cp /tmp/initrd.img-`uname -r` /boot/

Installing Time Synchronization Server

Since the cluster nodes will be sharing the root file system and various files and directories shall be common among them it is imperative that time be synchronized among the nodes. Otherwise timestamps on files may prompt irritating warning or even error messages when executing commands on the cluster nodes. The NTP package can be installed and configured on the boot server as follows:

1. Install NTP software package:

$ sudo aptitude install ntp

2. Adjust the configuration file /etc/ntp.conf as follows to allow cluster nodes to synchronize their time:

```
# /etc/ntp.conf #

restrict 10.1.1.0 mask 255.255.255.0 nomodify notrap
```

Setting up the NFS Server and Creating the Root File System

The NFS server provides the root file system to all cluster nodes. The root file system contains standard libraries and programs which may be used in our cluster. The packages for the NFS server are installed by issuing the command

```
$ sudo aptitude install nfs-kernel-server nfs-common
```

1. First we create a directory to store the bootable filesystem for cluster nodes

```
$ sudo mkdir /nfsroot/kerrighed
```

2. Next we edit **/etc/exports** by adding the following in order to export the the cluster nodes' root filesystem:

```
# /etc/exports #
/nfsroot/kerrighed 10.1.1.0/255.255.255.0(rw,no_subtree_check,async,no_root_squash)
```

3. For the NFS changes to take effect we re-export the file systems

```
$ sudo exportfs -avr
```

4. We have shared the root filsystem using NFS but so far it is empty. Now we populate it with a usable file system. We install the packages needed and install the base system to the bootable filesystem folder. In this case it is a minimal install of Ubuntu Jaunty (9.04).

```
$ sudo aptitude install debootstrap
debootstrap --arch i386 jaunty /nfsroot/kerrighed http://archive.ubuntu.com/ubuntu/
```

5. Change the current root of the file system to the bootable filesystem directory.

```
$ sudo chroot /nfsroot/kerrighed
```

All of the following commands are executed within the chrooted file system.

6. Set the root password using the standard command

```
$ passwd
```

It may be noted that the use of sudo facility is not done within the chrooted filesystem. This is so because once in the chrooted file system the user identity is that of root user and the use of sudo is not required to execute privileged commands.

7. Mount the **/proc** directory of the current machine

```
$ mount -t proc none /proc
```

The /proc is a pseudo file system used by the Linux kernel to store its run-time data structures. Several of following commands would not work correctly if /proc file system was not available while in the chrooted environment.

8. The base root filesystem created in the steps above by debootstrap is missing certain langauge files. These will cause to give warning and error messages intermittently. The missing files can be installed by issuing the command:

```
$ aptitude install language-pack-en
```

9. Edit /etc/apt/sources.list in order to download the necessary packages. This file identifies the upstream respositories to be used for automatic software installation.

```
# /etc/apt/sources.list #
deb http://archive.canonical.com/ubuntu jaunty partner
deb http://archive.ubuntu.com/ubuntu/ jaunty main universe restricted multiverse
deb http://security.ubuntu.com/ubuntu/ jaunty-security universe main multiverse restricted
deb http://archive.ubuntu.com/ubuntu/ jaunty-updates universe main multiverse restricted
deb-src http://archive.ubuntu.com/ubuntu/ jaunty main universe restricted multiverse
deb-src http://security.ubuntu.com/ubuntu/ jaunty-security universe main multiverse restricted
deb-src http://archive.ubuntu.com/ubuntu/ jaunty-updates universe main multiverse restricted
```

10. We need to update the current package listing for the cluster root filesystem thus:

```
$ aptitude update
```

11. Install the packages that our cluster nodes need for the DHCP, NFS and Secure Shell.

```
$ aptitude install dhcp3-common nfs-common nfsbooted openssh-server
```

12. Edit /etc/fstab of the bootable filesystem to have entries for proc and NFS mounted root filesystems.

```
# /etc/fstab #
#
# <file system> <mount point> <type> <options> <dump> <pass>
proc        /proc      proc defaults   0   0
/dev/nfs    /          nfs  defaults   0   0
```

13. Edit /etc/hosts and add all cluster nodes and server to it. In our case it would look like the following:

```
# /etc/hosts #
127.0.0.1 localhost

10.1.1.111   bootserver
10.1.1.221 kerrighednode1
10.1.1.222 kerrighednode2
10.1.1.223 kerrighednode3
10.1.1.224 kerrighednode4
```

14. Do the following to create a symlink to automount the NFS shared filesystem at startup. This should not collide with other existing services e.g./etc/rcS.d/S35xxxxxxx

```
$ In -sf /etc/network/if-up.d/mountnfs /etc/rcS.d/S34mountnfs
```

15. It is necessary to edit **/etc/network/interfaces** and disable the network manager from managing the nodes ethernet cards, as it can cause issues with NFS. Change the network configuration to be manual as shown below:

```
# /etc/network/interfaces #
# Used by ifup(8) and ifdown(8). See the interfaces(5) manpage or
# /usr/share/doc/ifupdown/examples for more information.

# The loopback network interface
auto lo
iface lo inet loopback

# The primary network interface, commented out for NFS root
iface eth0 inet manual
```

In our case the network interface is configured during the kernel booting by the DHCP client within the Linux Kernel TCP/IP stack.

16. Create an administrative user for the bootable system. Replace <username> with whatever you want.

```
$ adduser <username>
```

17. Add an entry for the new user in the **/etc/sudoers** file. This will allow the user to perform administrative commands in the bootable file system.

```
# /etc/sudoers #
#User privilege specification
root ALL=(ALL) ALL
<username> ALL=(ALL) ALL
```

18. Install the NTP software for time synchronization:

```
$ sudo aptitude install ntpdate
```

19. Add the following to /etc/default/ntpdate for time to be synchronized with the Internet Standard NTP servers:

```
# The settings in this file are used by the program ntpdate-debian, but not
# by the upstream program ntpdate.

# Set to "yes" to take the server list from /etc/ntp.conf, from package ntp,
# so you only have to keep it in one place.
NTPDATE_USE_NTP_CONF=no

# List of NTP servers to use  (Separate multiple servers with spaces.)
# Not used if NTPDATE_USE_NTP_CONF is yes.
NTPSERVERS="ntp.pool.org"

# Additional options to pass to ntpdate
NTPOPTIONS=""
```

20. Add the following command to /etc/rc.local

```
# /etc/rc.local #

/usr/bin/ntpdate-debian
```

21. Exit from the chrooted bootable filesystem

```
$ exit
```

Testing the diskless boot system

In order to test the network based booting of cluster nodes we perform the following steps.

1. Restart the software providing boot services

```
$ sudo /etc/init.d/tftpd-hpa restart
$ sudo /etc/init.d/dhcp3-server restart
$ sudo /etc/init.d/nfs-kernel-server restart
```

2. Boot the cluster nodes after their MAC addresses have been enterted into the DHCP configuration. We would observe the boot time messages on the cluster nodes indicating each of the steps:

a. PXE Boot messages showing PXE, DHCP and TFTP activity

b. Kernel loading, hardware detection and initialization messages

c. NFS mounting of root filesystem

d. Starup of Linux services such as Secure Shell, Cron and others on the cluster node

3. The interaction between the boot server and the cluster nodes can also be observed on the boot server by watching the /var/log/syslog file on the boot server using the command:

```
$ tail -f /var/log/syslog
```

Now that we have got a diskless boot system setup, we need to build the Kerrighed kernel for the nodes to use and configure the Kerrighed settings in order to have a working SSI (Single System Image) cluster. Those steps are deatiled in the next section.

Building the Kerrighed Linux Kernel

These instructions are mostly based on [Kerrighed 2009] and are duplicated here with necessary clarifications. Current Kerrighed release is based on Linux Kernel 2.6.20. A version based on Linux Kernel 2.6.30 is in the making and is available through the git repository. That should give a huge leap forward to the Kerrighed project in terms of general Linux kernel compatibility. We proceed to the instructions on downloading and building Kerrighed and the pre-requisite software.

1. On the boot server, once again chroot into the bootable filesystem.

```
$ sudo chroot /nfsroot/kerrighed
```

2. Install the necessary packages for compiling the Kerrighed Linux Kernel into the bootable filesystem.

```
$ aptitude install automake autoconf libtool pkg-config gawk rsync bzip2 gcc-3.3 libncurses5
libncurses5-dev wget lsb-release xmlto patchutils xutils-dev build-essential
```

Above would install the GNU C/C++ compiler and other software building tools. Next we get the latest kerrighed sources from INRIA's GForge and the vanilla 2.6 kernel.

1.1.1   Installing Kerrighed from the Source

Following steps are taken to build Kerrighed from sources.

1. To get the Kerrighed sources from INRIA's Gforge use wget as follows:

```
$ wget -O /usr/src/kerrighed-latest.tar.gz http://kerrighed.gforge.inria.fr/kerrighed-latest.tar.gz
```

Another method is to obtain the latest source from Kerrighed subversion repository as shown below:

```
$ svn checkout svn://scm.gforge.inria.fr/svn/kerrighed/branches/kerrighed-2.4
```

2. Optionally, download linux-2.6.20 sources tarball into '/usr/src'. You can once again use the wget utility to perform the download.

```
$ wget -O /usr/src/linux-2.6.20.tar.bz2 http://www.kernel.org/pub/linux/kernel/v2.6/linux-2.6.20.tar.bz2
```

3. Decompress the downloaded Tarballs:

```
$ cd /usr/src
$ tar zxf kerrighed-2.4.0.tar.gz
$ tar jxf linux-2.6.20.tar.bz2
```

4. Configure the Sources:

```
$ cd kerrighed-2.4.0
$ ./configure
```

5. Configure the kernel:

Running ./configure sets up the kernel with a default configuration which may not suit your needs but gives you a running Kerrighed configuration. Use `./configure --help` for possible options.

6. Build the sources:

```
$ make
```

If you have more than one CPU core on the boot server you can use

```
$ make -j 4
```

to increase the speed of compilation by initiating four instances of compiler processes. After the kernel is compiled you can go ahead and install all, as user **root**

```
$ make install
```

To confirm if everything has been installed properly you can check the installation. You should now have the following dir/files installed as shown in Table 2.

Table 2: Kerrighed files installed

File	Purpose
/boot/vmlinuz-2.6.20-krg	Kerrighed kernel
/boot/System.map	Kerrighed kernel symbol table
/lib/modules/2.6.20-krg	Kerrighed modules
/etc/init.d/kerrighed	Kerrighed service script *
/etc/default/kerrighed	Service configuration
/usr/local/share/man	Manpages
/usr/local/bin/krgadm	Cluster administration tool
/usr/local/bin/krgcapset	Process capabilities tool
/usr/local/bin/krgcr-run	Process checkpoint/restart helper
/usr/local/bin/migrate	Process migration tool
/usr/local/lib/libkerrighed-*	Kerrighed library
/usr/local/include/kerrighed	Kerrighed library headers

Kerrighed Configuration

The Kerrighed kernel needs one parameter, the session id. This id is between 1 and 254 and can be set through either the Kernel boot command line or through a configuration file /etc/kerrighed_nodes. Each instance of a Kerrighed cluster within the same network has a unique session_id. This allows Kerrighed cluster nodes to identify their siblings within the same cluster. If using the Kernel boot command line the boot parameter would be session_id=XX (XX is between 1 and 254 and same for all nodes within the same Kerrighed cluster). Alternatively, if using the second method edit the /etc/kerrighed_nodes file to define the session ID for all nodes of the cluster, and the number of nodes that have to be available before the cluster autostarts. It should look like the following:

```
# /etc/kerrighed_nodes #
session=1  #Value can be 1 - 254
nbmin=4    #Number of nodes which load before kerrighed autostarts.
```

If nbmin is set to 0 the cluster would not start automatically and would have to be manually started.

Edit the file /etc/default/kerrighed and ensure that it contains the following so the kerrighed service is loaded and started within the Kernel of a clsuter node:

```
# /etc/default/kerrighed #
# If true, enable Kerrighed module loading
ENABLE=true
```

Issue the following command so that dynamic libraries installed by Kerrighed are registered with the dynamic library loader within the cluster node root filesystem:

```
$ ldconfig
```

Exit the chrooted bootable filesystem

```
$ exit
```

Now we must reconfigure the TFTP boot configuration we set up earlier to use the Kerrighed kernel. First, copy the new Kerrighed kernel to the tftp directory.

```
$ cp /nfsroot/kerrighed/boot/vmlinuz-2.6.20-krg /var/lib/tftpboot
```

Edit /var/lib/tftp/pxelinux.cfg/default so it boots the Kerrighed kernel. It should looks like:

```
LABEL linux
KERNEL vmlinuz-2.6.20-krg
APPEND console=tty1 root=/dev/nfs nfsroot=10.1.1.111:/nfsroot/kerrighed ip=dhcp rw
```

Since all the configuring is done its time to restart the servers again.

```
$ sudo /etc/init.d/tftpd-hpa restart
$ sudo /etc/init.d/dhcp3-server restart
$ sudo /etc/init.d/nfs-kernel-server restart
```

Once again boot up all of the nodes, and if the login prompt appears, the new kernel has booted fine. Login into one of the nodes (either by ssh or on the node itself).

Starting Kerrighed

You can check if all nodes in the cluster are up and running by typing:

```
$ sudo krgadm nodes
```

You should see a list of all nodes in the format node_id:session. In our case we should see the following:

```
101:1 102:1 103:1 104:1
```

To start the kerrighed cluster type

```
$ sudo krgadm cluster start
```

To see if the cluster is running type the following:

```
$ sudo krgadm cluster status
```

To list the process capabilites for the kerrighed cluster type:

```
$ sudo krgcapset -s
```

To allow process migration to take place between nodes in the cluster type the following:

```
$ sudo krgcapset -d +CAN_MIGRATE
```

Hopefully, by this point the Kerrighed cluster should be working nicely. To see if it is working try running top from the command line and pressing 1 to list all the CPUs in the cluster. Don't worry if they have strange IDs, as its to do with the Kerrighed autonumbering implementation. You can also check the process migration is working from top by starting a number of long running CPU intensive processes, and seeing if all CPUs listed reach 100% usage.

Testing Kerrighed

In order to test Kerrighed we use the building of Linux Kernel as a processing intensive task. First we build the Linux Kernel using single process and then by using large number of concurrent processes. Table 3 below shows the results:

Table 3: Kerrighed performance on compiling Linux kernel

Run Number	Number of Processes	Kerrighed Process Migration Enabled	Time (sec)
1	1	No	537
2	2	No	286
3	4	No	246
4	4	Yes	412
5	8	No	523
6	8	Yes	401
7	16	No	530
8	16	Yes	410
9	24	No	538
10	24	Yes	Hangs/Crashes
11	48	No	Fails (Out of Memory)
12	48	Yes	Hangs/Crashes

Results presented in Table 3 require some explanation. We ran trials with number of concurrent kernel compilation processes to be 1, 2, 4, 8, 16, 24 and 48. For each number of concurrent processes except 1 and 2 concurrent processes we ran the kernel building make command with both the Kerrighed process migration disabled as well as enabled. It can be seen as the number of concurrent compilation processes increases, the instances where Kerrighed process migration is in effect require lesser time. Overall there is   better performance with Kerrighed process migration but the overheads of inter-node communication make the instances where the 1, 2 and 4 concurrent processes are used within the same cluster node to outperform those cases where process migration is in effect. This can be explained as follows. Kernel building process is sort of random and irregular, successive files do not require same amount of compilaton times. It does not reflect the structure of many scientific computation scenarios where there may be a lot of regularity in the algorithm. Nonetheless this exercise does demonstrate the capability of Kerrighed to migrate processes automatically and perform load levelling. With large number of kernel compile processes we see that the Kerrighed software hangs. Several issues related to instability of Kerrighed have been reported in Kerrighed developers forum. We were running the latest Kerrighed software on 64 bit platform. It appears that more work is required to get Kerrighed stable. Another explanation of kernel compile hanging the cluster could be race conditions arising due to Kerrighed scheduler. In the figure 10 we show the concurrent compilation processes and corresponding CPU utilizations within the cluster nodes.

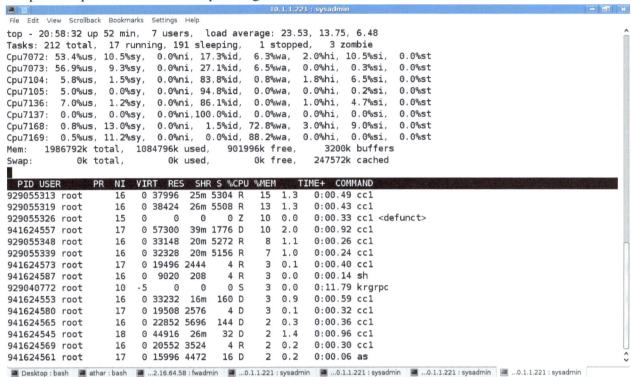

Fig. 10. CPU utilization with concurrent Linux kernel compilation processes

APPLICATION OF CLUSTERS TO SOLVE THE INTEGER FACTORIZATION PROBLEM (IFP)

The RSA public key cryptosystem was discovered in 1978 by three MIT professors, Ronald Rivest, Adi Shamir and Lenoard Adleman. Over the last three decades RSA and its variants have become the most widely implemented public key cryptographic scheme. The RSA algorithm is briefly presented below. It is assumed that Alice and Bob are two users who want to use RSA to protect their information.

Key Generation (Done independently by Alice and Bob and once only)

1. Choose two large random prime numbers p and q

2. Calculate $n = p \times q$

3. Calculate $\varphi(n) = (p-1) \times (q-1)$

4. Choose d such that d is co-prime with $\varphi(n)$, i.e. $\gcd(d, \varphi(n)) = 1$

5. Calculate $e = d^{1} \bmod \varphi(n)$

6. Publish $\{e, n\}$ as the public key and keep d secret as the private key.

Encryption/Decryption

To encrypt a message M for Alice, Bob will use Alice's public key $\{e, n\}$ and generate the encrypted version called the ciphertext C:

$$C = M^e \bmod n$$

Once Alice received the ciphertext C, she can recover the original message M as follows:

$$M = C^d \bmod n$$

The security of RSA algorithm lies in the adversary not being able to factor the publicly known modulus n. If the enemy were able to factor n, it could recover d from the publicly known e by using the equation in step 5 section 8.1. Hence RSA can be completely broken if there was a feasible way to factor an integer. For this reason RSA parameters p and q are chosen to be large integers, several hundred decimal digits long or equivalently several thousand binary digits long.

Over centuries attention has been paid to integer factorization (IF) problem. The best methods discovered so far require computationally infeasible amount of time for integers which are more than 200 decimal digits long. Table 4 is taken from [Aoki 2006] and shows the time complexity of the various integer factorization algorithms.

Table 4. Time Complexity of Various Integer Factorization Algorithms

method	complexity	effective range
TD	$L_P[1,1]$	$p \leq 2^{28}$
ECM	$L_P[1/2, 1.414]$	$p \leq 2^{130}$
MPQS	$L_N[1/2, 1.020]$	$N \leq 2^{320}$
SNFS	$L_N[1/3, 1.526]$	$N > 2^{320}$
GNFS	$L_N[1/3, 1.923]$	$N > 2^{320}$
MPGNFS	$L_N[1/3, 1.902]$	$N > 2^{2000}(?)$

$$L_x[s, c] = \exp((c + o(1))(\log x)^s (\log \log x)^{1-s})$$

One of the best known integer factorization algorithms is the Quadratic Sieve (QS) and its variants. The scheme for implementing integer factorization algorithm such as quadratic sieve using distributed processing of a cluster would use a structure as shown figure 11:

The QS algorithm consists of a number of steps and some of the steps involved lend themselves to parallel implementation. These are the steps that can be sped up using a cluster. However, other steps are of a nature that will not benefit by the cluster. One of the well known and well maintained implementation of QS and few other IF algorithms is available in [Msieve 2009].

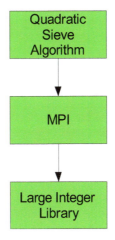

Fig. 11. General Structure of Parallel Integer Factorization Program Using Clusters

We have factored the following 103 decimal digit integer by using msieve implementation of QS. We show screen shot of 8 concurrent msieve processes running on the cluster in figure 12.

```
                                      10/1.1.221   wtadnin                                    _ ☐ ✕
 File  Edit  View  Scrollback  Bookmarks  Settings  Help
 top    20:58:32 up  52 min.  7 users    Load average: 23.53. 13.75. 1.48
 Tasks: 135 total     9 running. 126 sleeping.    0 stopped.    0 zombie
 Cpu7072: 11.6%us.86.7%sy. 0.0%ni. 0.0%id. 0.0%wa. 0.3%hi. 1.3%si. 0.0%st
 Cpu7073:100.0%us. 0.0%sy. 0.0%ni. 0.0%id. 0.0%wa. 0.0%hi. 0.0%si. 0.0%st
 Cpu7104: 96.7%us. 0.7%sy. 0.0%ni. 0.7%id. 0.0%wa. 0.0%hi. 2.0%si. 0.0%st
 Cpu7105:100.0%us. 0.0%sy. 0.0%ni. 0.0%id. 0.0%wa. 0.0%hi. 0.0%si. 0.0%st
 Cpu7136:100.0%us. 0.0%sy. 0.0%ni. 0.0%id. 0.0%wa. 0.0%hi. 0.0%si. 0.0%st
 Cpu7137:100.0%us. 0.0%sy. 0.0%ni. 0.0%id. 0.0%wa. 0.0%hi. 0.0%si. 0.0%st
 Cpu7168: 93.0%us. 0.7%sy. 0.0%ni. 5.0%id. 0.0%wa. 0.0%hi. 1.3%s  0.0%st
 Cpu7169: 99.7%us. 0.0%sy. 0.0%ni. 0.3%id. 0.0%wa. 0.0%hi. 0.0%si. 0.0%st
 Mem:    1986792k total,    604008k used.  1382784k free.     4800k buffers
 Swap:        ok total,         ok used.        ok free.   204108k cached

   PID USER     PR  NI  VIRT  RES   SHR S \CPU  \MEM    TIME+   COMMAND
 929041145 root      25  0 43088  31m  212 R  100  1.6  1:23.44 msieve
 929041147 root      25  0 49020  39m  556 R  100  2.0  1:16.42 msieve
 937429548 root      25  0 41036  29m  772 R  100  1.5  0:19.09 msieve
 929041146 root      25  0 48868  37m  388 R  100  2.0  1:17.70 msieve
 929041148 root      25  0 41864  30m  772 R  100  1.6  1:19.88 msieve
 929041149 root      25  0 41520 4636  120 R   99  0.2  1:09.58 msieve
 933235270 root      25  0 42792  24m  184 R   98  1.3  0:15.66 msieve
 929041144 root      25  0 43120  26m  184 R   93  1.3  1:16.34 msieve
 929040772 root      10 -5     0    0    0 S    0  0.0  0:03.70 krgrpc
 929040773 root      10 -5     0    0    0 S    0  0.0  0:03.40 krgcom/o
     1 root      18  0  4096  780  504 S    0  0.0  0:00.32 init
     2 root      RT  0     0    0    0 S    0  0.0  0:00.00 migration/0
     3 root      34 19     0    0    0 S    0  0.0  0:00.00 ksoftirqd/0
     4 root      RT  0     0    0    0 S    0  0.0  0:00.00 watchdog/0
     5 root      RT  0     0    0    0 S    0  0.0  0:00.00 migration/1
 ☐ Desktop : bash  ☐ athw : bash  ☐ 2.16.64.58 twodnmn  ☐ 0.1.1.221 : ryadnmn  ☐ 0.1.1.221 : ryadnmn  ☐ 0.1.1.221 : ryadnmn  ☐ 0.1.1.221 : ryadnmn
```

Fig. 12. Multiple msieve processes performing sieving on the Kerrighed cluster

2792279122203516865820284555164126411588967906598302885660019469574081234567890121335890587924107811116

Factors generated with msieve using Quadratic Sieve algorithm are:

2 x 2 x 109 x 173 x 367 x 431 x 7573 x 504353 x 1997715487 x 22918009218061 x 133835033152975400607354515726890753138186867985471862847417

The time required to factor with and without the cluster is given in Table 5 below.

Table 5. Performance of QS Algorithm On 4 Node (8 CPU) Cluster

Number of Nodes	Number of CPUs	Time (seconds)	Speedup
1	1	124	1X
4	8	20	6X

By using the computational power of the cluster, the time consuming part of the QS algorithm, i.e., sieving is run in parallel with as many desired number of processes. Each process is responsible for generating only a fraction of the total number of relations which are required by the next stage of the QS algorithm. It is well known that the sieving is the computationally intensive part of the QS algorithm [Msieve 2009]. Once sufficient number of relations are thus developed using sieving the next stage of combining the relations is not time consuming and can be performed quickly even by a single cluster node.

CONCLUSION

We have been able to present the current state of Linux clustering technology and provide details on setting up a single server image cluster using the Kerrighed. We have seen that one possible application of Linux clusters is to break the RSA algorithm by factorizing the RSA modulus using parallelization offered by clusters. However, the problem of integer factorization using clusters is still not completely solved. Both aspects of it, i.e., clustering middleware as well as integer factorization software have to be further integrated to get the benefit of clusters in this application domain.

REFERENCES

[Bader 2001] D.A. Bader and R. Pennington, ``Cluster Computing: Applications," The International Journal of High Performance Computing, 15(2):181-185, May 2001.

[Gropp 2002] W. Gropp and E. Lusk, "Goals Guiding Design: PVM and MPI" Proc. IEEE Cluster 2002.

[HA-OSCAR 2003] High Availability Open Source Cluster Application Resources beta release http://xcr.cenit.latech.edu/ha-oscar/index.html accessed on July 27th, 2009.

[Kerrighed 2004] C. Morin, R. Lottiaux, G. Valle, P. Gallard, D. Margery, J. Berthou, and I. Scherson." Kerrighed and data parallelism: Cluster computing on single system image operating systems" Proc. of Cluster 2004. IEEE, September 2004.

[LAM/MPI 2008] LAM/MPI Parallel Computing, http://www.lam-mpi.org/ last accessed Aug 3, 2009.

[MPI Forum 2008] Message Passing Interface-2, MPI Forum http://www.mpi-forum.org/index.html accessed on July 25, 2009.

[MPICH2 2009] MPI Implementation latest version released July 2009 http://www.mcs.anl.gov/research/projects/mpich2/ accessed on Aug 3, 2009.

[OpenMPI 2009] Open MPI: Open Source High Performance Computing, http://www.open-mpi.org/ last accessed Aug 3, 2009.

[OpenSSI 2006] OpenSSI version 1.9.1 for Fedora core 3, http://openssi.org/cgi-bin/view?page=download.html accessed on July 27th 2009.

[OSCAR 2009] Open Source Cluster Application Resources release 6.0.3 May 2009 http://svn.oscar.openclustergroup.org/trac/oscar/wiki accessed on July 25th, 2009.

[PVM 1997] Parallel Virtual Machine-3.4 1997 http://www.csm.ornl.gov/pvm/pvm_home.html accessed on July 25, 2009.

[EBC 2009] Easy Ubuntu Clustering forum http://ubuntuforums.org/showthread.php?p=6495259 accessed on July 15, 2009.

[Kerrighed 2009] Kerrighed 2.4.0 Release Notes avilable at http://kerrighed.org/wiki/index.php/Installing_Kerrighed_2.4.0

[MOSIX 2009] MOSIX at Wikipedia, http://en.wikipedia.org/wiki/MOSIX

[sage-devel] Quadratic Sieve Timings + Request for help tuning by Bill Hart, Bill Hart, Sun, 03 Dec 2006

[Raymond 2003] The Art of Unix Programming, Eric Steven Raymond, Available at http://www.faqs.org/docs/artu.

[Top500a] Top500 Supercomputing Sites, Operating Family Share Over Time, Available at http://www.top500.org/overtime/list/33/osfam

[Top500b]   Top500   Supercomputing   Sites,   Interconnect   Family   Share   Over   Time,   Available   at
        http://www.top500.org/overtime/list/32/connfam

[OpenMosix 2009] The OpenMosix Project Web Page available at http://openmosix.sourceforge.net/

[OpenSSI 2009] OpenSSI (Single System Image) Clusters for Linux Website avilable at http://openssi.org/

[Aoki 2006] Integer Factoring Utilizing PC Cluster, Kazumaro Aoki, NTT Japan, Presentation at Workshop on Cryptographic
        Hardware and Embedded Systems - CHES 2006.

[Msieve 2009] Integer Factorization Source Code for Msieve at http://www.boo.net/~jasonp/qs.html

## CHAPTER 4

Wireless Sensor Networks: Fundamentals, Technology and Applications

Nassar Ikram, Shakeel Durrani, Hasan Sajid and Husnain Saeed

Dr_nassar_ikram@yahoo.com, {shakeel.durranii, hasan.sajid, husnain.saeed}@gmail.com
National University of Sciences & Technology (NUST) Pakistan

Abstract: Sensing makes us aware of our ambient environment with amazing precision and speed. The influx of multitude attributes is processed in real time that makes us act in an exceptionally coordinated and timely manner. This human capability has influenced researchers worldwide trying to imitate this intricate delicacy of nature. Such a concept of global sensing and actuation is what the world has been waiting for, which has emerged in the form of Wireless Sensor Networks (WSN). This chapter delves into the whole spectrum of WSNs; explaining in detail the constituents (sensors, processor, transceiver etc) of sensor node, characteristics, survey of existing platforms, network dynamics and topology, energy matters and applications of WSNs. Applications of WSN have been given special consideration to show how WSN can revolutionize living standards, safety and our environment concurrently being more economically beneficial. Extensive due diligence has been carried out to ensure the right technology for the right application, with comparison to existing solutions and supported by real life deployments. In the end, a macro level insight of emerging branches (WMSN and WSAN) of WSNs provides a glimpse into the future of WSN.

INTRODUCTION

There is a global push towards wireless rather than wire bounded systems in every aspect of technology, the cars we drive, our homes, buildings, industry are instrumented with innumerable wireless devices. This tendency has steered more research and investment in the fields of wireless technologies. Sensor networks have in the past existed as wired network; our houses, buildings and industries are full of conduits running through them often leading to different types of sensors and actuators such as temperature, humidity, infrared, fire alarms and light switches etc. They have been substantial in bringing automation concepts but have been unable to unlock the true nature of sensor networks.

Wired sensor networks offered highest form of reliability and security but not at an affordable cost. Albeit the cost of sensors and electronic items plummeted remarkably, challenges associated with the conduit layout, installation and maintenance plus shortcomings for different application requirements, make the sensor network an expensive and unsuitable solution.

Wireless sensor networks have been deemed suitable for most of the applications. WSN virtually eliminates long clusters of wires and bulky equipment. A typical WSN consists of spatially distributed nodes, forming mesh for information gathering and processing in a proactive and energy efficient manner. With state-of-the-art, low-power circuit and networking technologies, a node lasts for years with a 1% low duty cycle working mode.

WSN trademarks diverse features such as proactive nature, mesh architecture, ubiquitous deployment, self – configuration, energy efficiency, autonomous and unattended operation and low cost solution make them obvious choice over wired networks. WSNs are a major shift from interactive towards proactive computing, preempting unwanted events and intelligently taking actions on our behalf.

Against the brighter side of WSNs, there are some serious challenges such as reliability, standardization, energy scarcity and node size, demanding for new algorithms and protocols. Fortunately, these issues have been successfully addressed to industry satisfaction with reliability achievements up to 99.9%, emergence of low power communication standards such as Zigbee [1] and development of low cost and low power sensors, transceivers and processors.

The enormous impact and potentials of WSNs have already been realized, how these tiny nodes can transform industries - agriculture, environment to manufacturing, military, health and medicine. Envisaging, sensors buried in soil can help ameliorate crops quality and production, smart smoke detection network can actively guide fire fighters to evacuate trapped victims and extinguish fire, smart nodes turning our homes into smart homes creating pleasant climate with reduced utility bills are few of infinite possibilities this technology offers.

In this chapter, we introduce WSN technology, groomed from basics to real life applications for ease of understanding. Consistent with application perspective, it provides macro-level insight of WSNs. Following section provides an insight into sensor node, the basic building block of WSN, section 3 comprises of a survey of existing platforms. Section 4 encompasses the characteristics of WSNs followed by real life applications in section 5. In the end, a brief summary of two emerging branches Wireless Multimedia Sensor Networks (WMSN) and Wireless Sensor and Actor Networks (WSAN) of WSN are discussed to provide a glimpse into future of WSN.

Composition of WSN

Wireless sensor network comprises of innumerable interacting sensor nodes pervasively deployed in a sporadic manner. Sensor nodes form building blocks of WSNs, comprising of an efficient processor, an energy source such as battery, an ultra low power transceiver for communication and sensors for perceiving its surrounding.

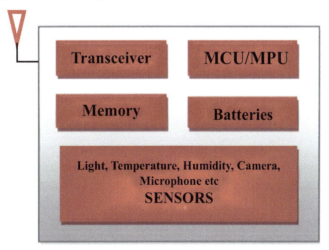

Fig.1. A typical Sensor Node

The subsequent subsections provide macro-level insight from an application perspective into characteristics and developments made so far for each component of a sensor node.

Microprocessor/ Microcontroller Unit

Microprocessors (MPU) / Microcontrollers (MCU), the computational hub serves as the brain of sensor nodes. Each MPU/MCU comprises of an underlying operating system. MPU/MCU is responsible for

(a) Perceiving physical world characteristics through   sensing,
(b) Analysis and extraction of requisite data,
(c) Emanation and timely execution of commands to respective actuators,
(d) Streaming of desired data and inter node communication and
(e) Optimization of energy sources through power management strategies.

Both MCU and MPU are used in nodes as per the scope of the node for which it is built. A plethora of state of the art MCU and MPU in market makes the selection a tedious job. Highly integrated processors with on-board peripherals often including software-controlled clock management capabilities reducing power consumption by inactive peripherals and peripheral controllers have made our task easier. The selection of the unit is marked by some other important computational parameters as well, listed hereunder:

* Processor Clock Speed
* Memory
* Size
* Peripherals
* Cost
* Peripheral Power consumption
* 8/16/32 bit addressable
* Power Management via multiple operation states (normal, idle, slow clock, standby etc)

The parameters above form a good basis for selecting MCU/MPU for any given application. Commercial Off The Shelf (COTS) MCUs/MPUs such as Intel's 32 bit Marvel PXA 271 processor used in Imote2 platform, 8 – bit Atmel's Atmega 128L used in MicaZ and other range of Atmel's 32 – bit MCU/MPU with built-in power management controllers such as AT91SAM9XE series are appropriate candidates to chose from.

Power is a critical factor that determines long term success of a WSN. Though power consumption in computation is less as compared to sensing and communication (in range of milli-watt when active and micro-watts when in standby mode), the unit still has to ensure excellent peripheral coordination and control for minimizing consumption. Power consumption (p) is proportional to frequency (f) and to the square of voltage (v) as shown by relationship 1 [2].

$$P \propto fv^2 \quad (1)$$

Recent advances in processor design techniques have led to the development of systems that support dynamic power management strategies based on Dynamic voltage scaling (DVS) technique that varies the supply voltage and clock frequency depending on the computation load without affecting the desired performance. DVS has been demonstrated as one of the most effective low power system design techniques reducing the consumption between 36% to 79%, thus making it ideal for energy constraint real time systems [3].

Operating Systems

The traditional OSs designed for operation between application software and hardware such as PC requires plenty of resources. There are embedded OSs as well but none of these meet the requirements of WSNs. Traditional OSs are designed to manage processes, memory, CPU time, file system, and devices. In contrast, WSN OS is influenced by resource constraints (power, memory and computational power), and data centric applications in addition to variable topology. There are several parameters that should be kept in mind while developing or selecting an OS for WSN applications which include the following:

- Energy efficient process management and scheduling.
- Memory management.
- Portability and support for hardware.
- Event driven Kernel model.
- Modular and general API for rapid deployment and application development.
- Real / Non-Real time operation requirements.
- Multitasking.
- Support for power management features to increase lifetime and performance.

A survey of existing WSN OSs is summarized in table 1 based on [4], [5], and [6].

Table.1 Comparison of WSN OSs

	TinyOS	SOS	Contiki	MANTIS OS	Nano-RK
Execution Model	Event Based	Event Based	Event + Thread	Thread Based	Real Time OS
Architecture	Monolithic	Modular	Modular	Modular	
Memory Requirement			2KB RAM and 40KB ROM	500 Bytes + 14KB Flash	2KB RAM + 18KB ROM
Dynamic Reprogramming	Application Level	Modular/ Component Level	Modular/ Component Level	Modular/ Component Level	
Scheduling	Non Real-time	Non Real-time	Non Real-time	Non Real-time	Real-time
Power management	Yes	Not explicit	Not explicit	Yes	Yes
Supported Platforms	Telos, Mica Mica2Dot, Mica2, MicaZ, Imote2	Mica2, MicaZ, Imote2, Cyclops	AVR MCU, MSP430, x86, 6502	Mica2, MicaZ, Telos	Firefly node

Microsoft has recently joined the race for providing a new entry in the form of a bootable runtime module with a small memory footprint of 300KB only. This new entrant is dubbed as ***Dot Net Micro framework*** [7] after its earlier ancestors for embedded applications such as Windows Embedded CE or Windows XP Embedded. It brings the benefits of .NET programming to resource constrained devices. In contrast to other varieties of .NET, it does not require an underlying operating system and combining rich managed code environment with native code interoperability. The primary goal of this new entrant, like its ancestors, is to remove hardware dependence. The framework currently supports Imote2 platform in addition to various other platforms.

The selection of an operating system for deploying a successful WSN entirely depends on the application, its domain (Industrial, military, health, environment etc) and requirements. For instance military and health applications require real time guarantees, environmental or remote monitoring may not require real time guarantee but optimal power conservation and scalability without degradation in network performance. Concluding, it is wholly dependent on application requirements to choose an OS based on the parameters mentioned above.

Radio Transceiver, Connectivity and Topology

Each node is equipped with a transceiver for communication. Most of the energy is consumed during communication in contrast to sensing and computation. In addition to severe resource constraints, these tiny nodes are most often deployed in a haphazard and random manner. This demands for ad hoc networking techniques; although many protocols and algorithms have been proposed for traditional wireless ad hoc networks, these are not well suited to the unique features and application requirements of sensor networks.
The diversity of domains for which wireless sensor networks can be employed makes it difficult to conceive a single solution as the requirements vary from application to application. Characteristics such as low cost, energy efficiency, self configuration comes at the cost of low bandwidth and reduced data rate. This is not desirable in case of applications involving data intense content such as multimedia, which require more bandwidth at the expense of other parameters. This makes single solution, a daunting or rather impossible task. For simplicity, we classify applications based on the data content (bandwidth), first set of applications with scalar data requiring low bandwidth and second set of applications involving data rich multimedia content. Reference to this section includes [4].

Numerously available COTS wireless technologies maximize the opportunity for a cost effective WSN solution. Wireless technologies such as WPAN, 3G, WLAN and Wi-Max can be considered for WSNs. A comparison of three major competitors for WSN application is illustrated in table 2 [8].

Applications requiring low power consumption, low data rate, reliability, ubiquitous connectivity and low cost, WPAN are the most feasible among the available COTS wireless technologies. WPAN technologies such as WirelessHART, Bluetooth, UWB and Zigbee have emerged recently. Their features include self configuring, self healing, energy awareness, low cost and mesh architecture. Ad hoc routing protocols are implemented using low power radios based on IEEE 802.15 standards. The IEEE 802.15 standards provides the lower layers of communication protocol stack (Physical and Media Access Control) with unique features as collision avoidance, real time guarantee and power management.

Table.2 Major Competitors for WSN application

Property	802.11	802.15.1/Bluetooth	802.15.4/ZigBee
Range (m)	~100	~10 to 100	~10
Data throughput (Mbps)	~2 to 54	~1 to 3	~0.25
Power consumption	Medium	Low	Ultralow
Battery life measured in:	Minutes to hours	Hours to days	Days to years
Size relationship	Large	Smaller	Smallest
Cost/complexity ratio	>6	1	0.2

Among WPAN technologies, Bluetooth (IEEE 802.15.1) technology was at first considered a possibility, but it was soon deemed unsuitable for resource constraint and cost effective solutions. For interior building applications, designers ruled out Wi-Fi (wireless fidelity, IEEE 802.11b) standards for sensors as being too complex and supporting more bandwidth than is actually needed for typical sensors. Zigbee has emerged as the most suitable and obvious choice for designers and research community.

Zigbee with its increasing acceptance and adaptation is on its way to becoming a leading wireless technology and standard for WSN low cost, energy constraint and mesh architecture applications. Zigbee supports maximum data rate of 250 kbps, offering rates as low as 20 kbps with lowest power requirement among its competitors (UWB, Bluetooth and WirelessHART). Zigbee supports mesh architecture providing a reliable and long range (30 to 250 ft) network operating in 2.4 GHz ISM band. Zigbee devices are designed to run several years on a single set of batteries, making them ideal candidates for unattended or difficult-to reach locations. Therefore, Zigbee focuses on commercial building and home automation, telecom applications, personal, home and hospital care etc as prospective application domains. Texas Instruments CC2420 [9] 802.15.4/Zigbee compliant radio and ATMEL's AT86RF231 [10] Transceiver chip for 802.15.4/Zigbee/6LoWPAN/ /WirelessHART are good examples of COTS transceivers for WSN applications.

Ultra Wide band radio has been of great interest recently for distributed sensor networks with its impressive features and capabilities. UWB is a short range technology that can penetrate walls making them an ideal indoor choice. The UWB transceivers offer increased bandwidth with capability to transmit 100 Mbps of data at a distance of 10m. Another important characteristic is a built-in time-of flight property that makes it very easy to measure ranges with resolution down to 1 cm with a range of 40m, thus providing a three in one solution for communication, tracking and localization. Depending on the usage cases, ZigBee and UWB technologies can either be complementary or overlapping [11].

Applications in the second set, which require high bandwidth and real time guarantees, wireless mesh networks can be implemented with various wireless technologies including IEEE

802.11a/b/g/n series of wireless LANs, the MAN-scope IEEE 802.16 (also known as WiMax), cellular technologies or combinations of more than one type.

Within-building WSNs now tend to look to use Zigbee/IEEE802.15.4 while WSNs that are in the open (outside buildings and over a broad geography) may also find these technologies useful.

In particular, IEEE-based wireless LAN standards have been given consideration. IEEE 802.11a/b/g/n is a collection of related technologies that operate in the 2.4-GHz ISM band, the 5-GHz ISM band, and the 5-GHz UNII bands; it provides the highest power and longest range of the common unlicensed wireless technologies. Transmission data rates can reach 54 Mbps (twice as much with the latest IEEE 802.11n protocol). The new WiMax standard (IEEE 802.16) may also be useful for metropolitan environments, as is the application of cellular third-generation technologies. IEEE 802.11 seems to be more promising with its increased range, high data rates but at the cost of reduced lifetime and size.

WSN802G [12] wireless sensor network module is one of the latest arrivals at the time of writing this chapter offering high data rates up to 2 Mbps with output power of 10 dBm. WLNB-AN-DP101Airborne™ 802.11b [13] Wireless LAN Node Module is another module offering data rates of up to11 Mbps with output power of 15 dBm but at the cost of increased size and power consumption.

Despite the availability of various wireless technologies, applications most often rely on heterogeneous networks including WSN in combination with Wi-Fi /GPRS/GSM technology as shown in figure 2.

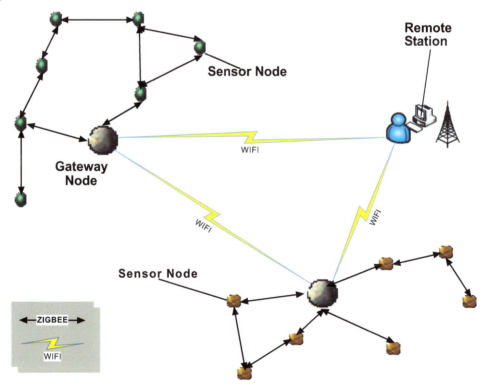

Fig. 2. Heterogeneous WSN

Sensor Transducers

One of the most important tasks of WSN is extracting desired information from its environment. This is done using various sensors, thereby interpreting sensor measurements into meaningful environmental features [14]. Sensors are devices used to convert physical quantity (light, temperature, pressure etc) into a measurable form as depicted in figure 3. Sensors are capable of measuring physical quantities like temperature, pressure, light, magnetic field, sound, heat etc. Due to very high applicability, sensors are extensively used in a variety of applications. The selection of sensors is based on certain factors such as accuracy, calibration, resolution, cost, repeatability, range etc [15].

Fig. 3. Sensor Workflow

Based on the operation, sensors can be classified into two broad categories:

a. *Active sensors* emit energy into the environment, and then measure the environmental reaction. Examples include ultrasonic range finders and laser range finders.
b. *Passive Sensors* measure ambient environmental energy entering the sensor. Examples include temperature probes, microphones and CCD or CMOS cameras. [14]

Wireless Sensor Network applications mostly require nodes to last for long durations. Active sensors continuously consume power to work whereas passive sensors only consume power in case of an event such as Passive Infra Red (PIR) Sensors activating a dormant system as soon as motion is detected. Passive sensors consume current in range of micro and in some cases nano amperes thereby conserving energy. The energy efficacy of passive sensors clearly makes passive sensors as an obvious choice for WSN applications.

Table 3 lists different sensors, classified based on stimulus:

Table 3. Sensor Transducers classification based on input

S/No	Stimulus	Types
1	Mechanical	• Pressure Sensors • Tunneling Sensors • Capacitive Sensors • Accelerometers
2	Magnetic and Electro-magnetic	• Hall effect sensors • Magnetic Field Sensors
3	Thermal	• Temperature Sensors
4	Optical	• Opto-couplers • Infrared Sensors
5	Chemical and Biological	• Chemi-resistors • Metal Oxide gas Sensors • Electrochemical transducers • Bio Sensors
6	Acoustic	• Microphone

Advances in Micro Electromechanical Systems (MEMS) and micro fabrication techniques have positively contributed in the field of sensors. MEMS sensors are by now very well developed and are available for most sensing applications in wireless networks. Many vendors now produce commercially available sensors of different types that are suitable for wireless network applications [11]. Examples include MEMS sensors from leading vendors such as STMicroelectronics, Akustica, National Instruments and Analog Devices offering MEMS sensors such as gyroscopes, accelerometers, temperature sensors and microphone etc. Envisaging, use of MEMS sensors will miniaturize the existing nodes with improved battery life.

BATTERIES AND RENEWABLE ENERGY SOURCES

Energy source is an integral part of a WSN, responsible for keeping electrons running for a sustainable and long lasting network performance. Sensor nodes have limited energy sources in form of batteries which are difficult and sometimes impossible to replace or replenish. This forms a major bottleneck in survival of a wireless sensor network. References for this section include [16] and [17].

Each of the nodes constituting a WSN requires energy for computation, sensing and communication. A lot of research and effort especially in micro domain has produced MEMS sensors, ultra low power transceivers and processors offering high performance with significantly reduced power requirements and size. These advancements along with energy cautious algorithms have optimized energy usage increasing lifetime of nodes but have not been successful in offering a permanent solution.

Unlike other issues, research efforts towards energy sources have been overlooked, as a result of which even most recent nodes such as Imote2 employs AAA size cells, increasing the size of the node by almost 80% and weight by 75%.

At present a two point modus operandi is envisaged for a permanent and sustainable solution to resolve energy crisis.

(a) *Economical use of available energy* from primary source such as a battery and secondly
(b) *Energy scavenging* using renewable energy sources (solar, wind, vibration etc) for continuous recharging of batteries.

Batteries offer limited time period based on consumption and therefore require recharging or replacement which is not possible in most cases. Table 4 illustrates commercially available cells with their capacity [18].

Table 4. Commercially Available Cells

Cell Size	Capacity (mAH)
AAA	700
AA	1500-2000
C	5000
D	9000-12000
9V	550

Energy scavenging using ambient energy seems to be a promising solution for pervasively deployed WSN. In pursuit of a suitable and permanent solution, a number of renewable energy sources with respective power densities are in table 5 [19]:

Table 5. Power densities of various harvesting technologies

Harvesting technology	Power density
Solar cells (outdoors at noon)	$15mW/cm^3$
Piezoelectric (shoe inserts)	$330\mu W/cm^3$
Vibration (small microwave oven)	$116\mu W/cm^3$
Thermoelectric (10° C gradient)	$40\mu W/cm^3$
Acoustic noise (100dB)	$960nW/cm^3$

So far research and efforts concentrated for renewable energy extraction have not shown any remarkable development and outcome. Solar energy is fast becoming as primary source of renewable energy because of its ubiquitous availability. Least variations in solar energy offer consistent output voltage, which as a result, simplifies interface circuitry between the source and electronic circuitry. Concepts such as Solar Biscuit [12] is one such example, it acquires ambient solar energy and salvages it into a super capacitor with capability to accumulate charge many times than a simple capacitor.

CHARACTERISTICS OF A TYPICAL WSN

In contrast to conventional networks, WSNs are unique in terms of its characteristics and features. Some of the main characteristics of WSN are:

- *Ubiquitous deployment*: The sturdy and resilient nature of network offers ubiquitous deployment irrespective of deployment issues and environmental factors. This characteristic makes them fit for remote, hazardous and inaccessible areas.
- *Network Density:* Unlike conventional networks, WSNs are highly dense networks comprising of large clusters of nodes ranging from hundreds to thousands.
- *Intelligence:* On board processing helps in analyzing the acquired data and then extracting the requisite information in an intelligent manner. This helps to curb relaying of raw and unnecessary data to center whereas in other networks continuous streaming of data makes system inefficient and unintelligent.
- *Coverage:* Each node in the network in addition to its role also acts as a router thereby ensuring connectivity of far away nodes. This results in a power efficient reliable network with increased coverage area and range.
- *Lifetime:* WSNs are expected to last from months to years with energy conserving and scavenging strategies as key to survival. Lifetime of a WSN varies from application to application.
- *Disposability:* A network once deployed especially in inaccessible areas, sometimes need not to be retrieved due to physical limitations. In such scenarios, the economics of a WSN makes it disposable instead of hefty conventional solutions.
- *Application Diversity:* WSNs offer wide area of applications as opposed to application specific networks.

- *Self configuring:* WSN most often supports mesh topology based on ad hoc networking protocols, featuring self management features. This intrinsic self management makes WSN resilient to continuously changing network topology, dynamics and node failures. This feature makes WSNs to stand out against other conventional networks.

- *Unattended Operation:* WSNs support round the clock unattended operations especially for networks deployed in hazardous and inaccessible areas without any human assistance.

- *Distributed operation:* Each and every node constituting a WSN is autonomous. These nodes put their act together to perform and share onus to accomplish their task. This distributed architecture minimizes the risk of network failure and shows resilience of network to node failures or malfunctioning.

- *Economical:* WSNs are highly *energy conserving*, low power and *cost effective* solutions for demanding requirements. The frugality starts right from low power and low cost COTS component selection to multi – state (normal, idle, sleep) network operation keeping network dormant for most of its lifetime.

- *Data Centric:* Unlike traditional networks, WSNs are data centric and not address based which implies that WSNs are based on data attributes (temperature, pressure etc) rather than unique identifiers. Therefore, WSNs are tailored for sensing and application tasks.

Existing Platforms

This section provides a survey of extensively used WSN platforms developed and employed by researchers worldwide for numerous applications, illustrated in table 6.

Table.6 Comparison of prominent existing WSN platforms application

S/No	Sensor Node	MCU/MPU	Transceiver	Program/Data Memory	OS/Framework Support	Applications
1	ECO Node [20]	DW8051	nRF24E1 2.4 GHz 1 Mbps	512 byte ROM 4 Kilo byte RAM 32 K EEPROM	N/A	Medicine, environmental monitoring, ambient intelligence
2	IMote 2.0 [21]	Marvel PXA 271 ARM 11-400 MHz	TI CC2420 2400-2483.5 MHz 250 Kb/s	32 MB Flash 32 MB SDRAM	TinyOS, LINUX, SOS and DOT NET Micro Framework	Digital Image Processing, condition base maintenance, industrial monitoring and analysis, seismic and vibration monitoring
3	MicaZ [22]	Atmel Atmega 128L	TI CC2420 2400-2483.5 MHz 250 Kb/s	128 Kb Flash	TinyOS, SOS, Mantis OS,	Indoor building monitoring and security, acoustic, video, vibration and other high speed sensor data
4	TelosB [23]	TI MSP430	IEEE 802.15.4/ZigBee Transceiver 2400-2483.5 MHz 250 Kbps	48 K Flash 10 Kb RAM	Contiki, TinyOS, SOS and Mantis OS	Platform for low power research development, wireless sensor network experimentation
5	Fleck 3B [24]	Atmel Atmega 1281	Nordic RF905 433/915 MHz 50 Kbps	128 Kb Flash 8 Kb RAM	Fleck Operating System	Marine Sensor Networks, Habitat monitoring

APPLICATIONS OF WIRELESS SENSOR NETWORKS

The magic of WSN has no doubt revolutionized our lives in almost all fields of life. A CEO of a multinational company while sitting in his office manages other facilities in Asia or Europe besides taking care of his home. A doctor while at home keeps check of patient's vitals round the clock with ease, farmer while sitting in the warmth of his abode manages crop yield, these are few of infinite examples of how WSNs will affect and become part of our lives.

The applications falling in this domain are characterized by their low bandwidth, data rates and power requirements.

Body Sensor Networks is emerging as major contributor in improving healthcare facilities and lifestyle of people. A typical body sensor network is constituted of small wireless physiological sensors connected to a PDA providing ubiquitous connectivity with the base station. As evident from the name, these networks are dedicated in forming specialized networks consisting of physiological sensors for variety of applications ranging from health to sports.

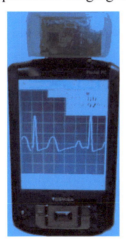

Fig. 4. Physiological sensor and PDA base station (Courtesy of Benny P.L. Lo, Imperial College London) [26].

Ubiquitous nature of these sensor networks help doctors in ambulatory monitoring of patients, providing beforehand information for saving precious lives. These networks help in triage for ease of doctors and medical staff with increased efficacy in case of exigency. Home care has become easy as doctors now have real time update in case of vital anomaly of their patients as a precursor to major episode. It helps to locate patient in case of emergency for guidance to a nearby medical facility or dispatch an ambulance immediately. The same concept can be employed to elderly care home where most of aged people often suffer from multiple diseases at later stage of life.

In addition to healthcare, these tiny and feather weight sensors can be employed for fitness purposes such as self assessment, training of athletes to improve team performance and prosthetics for amputees.

CardioNet and BSN node are two examples of body sensor networks being employed. CardioNet provides a remote heart monitoring system where ECG signals are transmitted to a Personal

Digital Assistant (PDA) and then routed to the central server by using the cellular network [25][26]. BSN [26] node consists of wireless physiological (ECG strip, 3-lead ECG, SpO2) and context aware (accelerometer, temperature) sensors relaying data to the base station via Wi-Fi/GPRS using PDA.

In near future, it seems that these tiny sensor nodes will accompany us from baby cradle to elderly care homes.

Structure and Equipment Health Monitoring

Despite standard building codes and design methodologies adopted to ensure public safety, major events such as seismic activities, floods, severe environmental conditions and overloading results in deterioration of structures, sometimes leading to devastating incidents.

In pursuit to avoid such scenarios, tethered Structural Health Monitoring (SHM) systems exist. These traditional approaches consist of sensors tied to the repository through wires, producing reliable results but at high cost due to set up and labor-intensive nature of these techniques. Current SHM techniques can be classified into two types [27].

Local-based method involve screening structures to identify defects (cracks, yielding etc) at component level using non-destructive evaluation technologies such as ultrasonic inspection. Such methods are expensive as it requires trained professionals.

Global-based method involves detecting damages by recording changes in commercially available SHM nodes to external stimuli. Most often this system comprises of sensors tethered to data acquisition system. Such systems are highly expensive and some time impossible to deploy for large infrastructure (civil infrastructure) due to nodal density issues resulting in high costs.

Costs of such deployed structural health monitoring systems have reportedly been in the range of thousands of dollars which tend to grow faster than linearly. Examples include installment of 350 sensing channels on Tsing Ma suspension bridge in Hong Kong with an estimated expenditure of $8 Million [28]. The same problem lies in utilizing structure monitoring for large structures such as aircraft, vessels and ships.

With the context of SHM, WSN is being considered by the research community as a suitable and highly economical substitute to traditional methods. WSN will significantly reduce cost by eliminating the need of long and costly wires, low maintenance and installation costs with added advantage of increased nodal density, deployment flexibility and large physical coverage.

With its characteristics, it can be assumed that WSN will help to take care of civil infrastructure (buildings, bridges, dams, museums etc) and people by reporting anomalies, predicting lifetime of structures for public safety and timely warning to authorities against any catastrophe for possible evacuation. It will help to remotely monitor, secure and detect leakages or breakdown in long pipelines (oil, gas, water, sewage etc), minimizing financial losses and protecting environment from its negative impacts. It will help make transport infrastructure reliable than ever before by using WSN for roads, railroads, ships and airplanes. It will be very useful in preserving historical sites such as civilizations, castles and churches etc.

Binns [29] has presented a wireless sensor system developed by researchers at the University of Dayton, Ohio for bridge monitoring. The wireless monitoring system, called WISE (Wireless Infrastructure Evaluation System), can perform wireless monitoring of bridge structures using any type of analog sensor. Once installed upon a bridge, communication with the WISE system can be established with a laptop computer or an inspector's PDA. The advantage of WISE, besides the compatibility with any off-the-shelf sensors, is its ability to incorporate an unlimited number of sensor channels in the global monitoring system [30].

WSN will help to meet the acknowledged goals for structure monitoring such as detection, localization and estimation of damage plus lifetime of structure. In future, it will help analysts, researchers and structural engineers to study the response of structure to variations in detail than never before. Concluding, WSN for SHM is still in nascent stage offering endless possibilities.

Home and Building Automation

The existing automation systems being expensive are not popular among enterprises as a result of inadequate features and unsatisfactory performance offered at hefty price. Most of these systems are either wired or based on point-to-point wireless solutions. Wires add too much cost to the system due to installation and maintenance services with least flexibility whereas point-to-point wireless solutions are prone to connectivity failures due to tough RF environments.

Home and building automation will be one of the prime beneficiaries of this emerging technology. WSN technology can either be used independently or with already existing building automation standards [31] such as LonWorks, OPC, KNX, Modbus and BAC-net. This will not only ensure quick solution but also provide backward compatibility to existing automation solutions already installed. One such example is implementation of BAC-net on ESB nodes proving the possible implementation of these standards on resource constraint sensor nodes [31].

Typically, sensor nodes are heterogeneously equipped with different sensors, spatially distributed in and around the building at desired points. These nodes follow multi-hopping strategy to reach the local base station, most often connected to a remote server via GSM/GPRS network depending upon application requirements.

Home and building automation are meant for smart homes, schools, offices and hospitals etc. These are generally used for variety of purposes ranging from control of HVAC systems, indoor environmental monitoring, lighting system monitoring and control, energy management, supporting elderly and handicapped people and building security and access control to name a few.

WSN technology independent of or with existing building automation standards offers economical solution with various advantages over other solutions. It forms a 100% reliable multi-hop mesh network in and around buildings for connectivity unlike point-to-point solutions with increased coverage. Nodes can be easily added into the network providing ease for future expansion without hassle of reconfiguration. Each node along with its functionality acts as a router thereby making void the need for access points. The compact size of nodes makes them easily installable at unapproachable heights. Ubiquitous connectivity offers ease of deployment and scalability from small homes up to enterprise level multinational companies within no time. These networks offer low operation and maintenance cost in contrast to traditional solutions.

One of the added advantage in using WSN technology for building automation is the fact that these energy constraint devices might not have to worry about their battery health since energy supply is adequate in buildings resulting in a virtually eternal network.

Environment monitoring

Rapidly increasing population and human's interference into nature's ecosystem has posed mankind numerous challenges in the form of natural calamities, erosion, wildlife extinction and deforestation to name a few. Increasing global warming is multiplying these problems fast and need to be addressed forthwith.

Concentrated efforts and research has been carried out to cope up with environmental issues but have failed to do so because of challenges posed by its vastness, unpredictability and lack of technology. WSNs with its adaptability, portability, low power requirements and resilience to harsh environmental conditions are a perfect choice for innumerable environmental issues currently being faced globally.

Early warning systems can be deployed using low cost WSN technology especially in areas prone to seismic activities, maritime areas or areas near to volcanic mountainous regions. Such systems act as an early warning system, helpful in predicting earthquakes, volcanic eruption, floods, landslides and tsunami, minimizing colossal damages in terms of property and lives.

In 2005, a network was deployed on Volc´an Reventador in northern Ecuador. An array of 16 nodes equipped with seismo-acoustic sensors was deployed over 3 km. The system routed the collected data through a multihop network and over a long-distance radio link to an observatory, where a laptop logged the collected data. The responsible researchers state that in contrast with existing volcanic data acquisition equipment, the sensor modules are smaller, lighter, and consume less power. Moreover, the resulting spatial distribution greatly facilitates scientific studies of wave propagation phenomena and volcanic source mechanisms [32] [33].

Another such early warning system is deployed in Bangladesh for flood controlling and warning [32] [34].

Urban and industrial areas can be instrumented with sensor nodes. This technology will help environmental agencies to keep strict check & balance and control over emissions of poisonous gases and toxic wastes polluting the environment. Low cost nodes allow greater nodal density for large areas such as metropolitans providing more precision than before. Such efforts will not only be helpful in improving health of inhabitants with improved air and water quality but also be helpful in overcoming global warming and depletion of ozone layer due to increased pollutants in environment.

Trees are an integral part of ecosystem. These reservoirs are vanishing fast due to fire breakout or theft for financial gains. These woods can be instrumented with tiny wireless nodes to warn in case of fire breakout or theft. Therefore such networks can help authorities to curb theft and control fire in case of breakout more effectively and with much ease.

Habitat monitoring

Biologists, Scientists, Ecologists and wildlife officials spend their lives studying relationship of animals and organisms with their environment, their movements, breeding, diseases, life processes and behavior. Habitat monitoring is often marked by problems such as vast surveillance area, difficult terrains, harsh environmental conditions, long term requirement and infrastructure less environment. Traditional methods often employed are inconsistent, energy consuming, costly and invalid at times. WSNs are ideal for infrastructure-less environment and therefore deemed suitable for habitat monitoring. WSN offers many advantages over earlier techniques, it helps to monitor and track animals remotely without any human interference, which might otherwise produce unreliable results. It offers extended range at low cost without the need of any communication infrastructure. The sturdy and compact nodes make them unobtrusive for animals and flexible to withstand harsh environmental conditions. This revolution will help researchers to observe nature closely and preserve endangered species with more accurate and positive outcomes. Great Duck Island [35] and ZebraNet project [36] are good examples of deployed WSN for habitat monitoring.

Agricultural Monitoring

It remains uncertain whether available resources and technologies will be able to meet food requirements of mushrooming population. Unfortunately, one out of six people does not get enough food to be healthy and lead an active life [37]. This deficit of food is expected to widen especially in context of developing countries, where resource constraint farmers rely on conventional farming strategies. The environmental challenges such as soil degradation with time and water scarcity add to woes of these poor farmers resulting in unpredictable crop yield and quality.

WSN for agriculture, though still in its infancy, is promising with self-organizing capabilities and frugality. Instrumented with these nodes, land management will become easy, efficient and productive. These networks will enable farmers to monitor agricultural parameters such as air temperature, relative humidity, light, soil moisture, canopy density and location etc in real time. Availability of these parameters will help farmers in devising new strategies for efficient irrigation, analyzing arability, prevention of pest and diseases, sowing and harvest periods, and coping with up climate variations. The outcome will be resource optimization to maximize productivity while minimizing environmental and economical risks.

In Europe, the Lofar Agro project is a study of precision agriculture that focuses on tailored management of a crop. This involves monitoring soil, crop and climate conditions in a field, generalizing the result and providing a Decision Support System (DSS) for treatments or taking differential action such as real time variation of fertilizer or pesticide application. The DSS gathers information from a weather station and the wireless network. This is employed to map out a temperature and soil humidity distribution which is used to develop an effective strategy for controlling diseases such as Phytophthora [38] [39].

In California, Beckwith *et al* designed, deployed and analysed output of a large scale implementation of a wireless sensor network in a vineyard [39]. Analysis of sensor data allowed the prediction of pH, titratable acids and berry weight. Using wireless sensors, Beckwith and his colleagues were able to determine a 6 hour threshold after the onset of frost when a wine maker would need to take action to deal with a weather problem [40].

These examples show the credible future for deploying self-organizing wireless sensors in agriculture especially for developing countries.

WIRELESS MULTIMEDIA SENSOR NETWORKS (WMSN)

Wireless Multimedia Sensor Networks (WMSN) is a new breed of WSNs. These are networks of wirelessly interconnected devices that are able to ubiquitously retrieve multimedia (MM) content such as video and audio streams, still images, and scalar sensor data from the environment [41]. These networks, in addition to MM retrieval, involve storage, real time processing and data fusion from multiple sources. An excellent reference to this section is [42].

MM being data rich poses many challenges to WSNs in terms of high band width and application specific QoS requirements, multimedia coding techniques for compression, in- network processing and energy requirements.

WMSN are often deployed in multi-tier fashion, with scalar sensors forming the lower tier and activating upper tiers comprising of multi-resolution cameras in case of events of interest. This is clearly illustrated in figure 5.

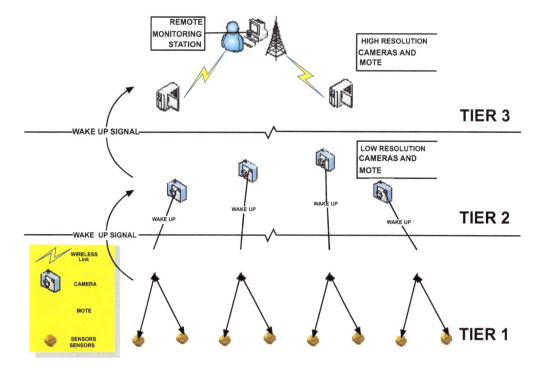

Fig. 5. Typical WMSN

This multi-tier approach in addition to energy conservation offers many advantages as listed below over traditional monitoring and surveillance networks:

(a) Distributed cameras provide multiple views of the same subject to overcome occlusion effect, this enlarges field of view.
(b) It offers redundancy which provides multiple views for understanding and analyzing ambiguous situations.
(c) Heterogeneous networks comprising of multi-resolution cameras can provide multi-resolution images from same point of view in regions of interest.

WMSNs offer wide range of applications augmenting human interaction with the physical world.

Security and Surveillance

Security and surveillance have become of prime importance globally. These MM nodes can be deployed over large geographical areas and inhospitable regions making them suitable for military purposes such as surveillance and reconnaissance. Law enforcement agencies can continuously monitor sensitive locations, public places, mega events and borders to curb terrorist activities and infiltration. Police department can use this technology to catch criminals and minimize crime rate.

WMSNs equipped with advanced digital signal processing techniques and intelligent algorithms can help to (a) identify and track subjects (criminals, vehicles) (b) perceive suspicious activities to notify the concerned authorities for timely action.

Traffic Monitoring and Control

It will be possible to monitor car traffic in big cities or highways and deploy services that offer traffic routing advice to avoid congestion. Multimedia sensors may also monitor the flow of vehicular traffic on highways and retrieve aggregate information such as average speed and number of cars. Sensors could also detect violations and transmit video streams to law enforcement agencies to identify the violator, or buffer images and streams in case of accidents for subsequent accident scene analysis. In addition, smart parking advice systems based on WMSNs will allow monitoring available parking spaces and provide drivers with automated parking advice, thus improving mobility in urban areas. [41]

In continuum of WSN applications, addition of MM can help assist in remote monitoring and assistance of patients with added advantage of audio and video. Furthermore audio and visual aids can greatly enhance environment and habitat monitoring.

WIRELESS SENSOR AND ACTOR NETWORKS (WSAN)

WSAN is a class of WSNs in which sensors and actors coexist via wireless medium. Sensors gather data from physical world whereas actors often known as actuators takes decisions based on acquired data from sensors and acts accordingly.

The coexistence of sensors and actors demands for *real time coordination* among actors as well as among sensors and actors. Such challenges require development of new algorithms and protocols for WSANs, in contrast to that for WSNs. Typically, WSAN are expected to follow two types of architecture for communication and coordination:

(a) **Automated**
   The data acquired by sensors is relayed to actors directly which process the data to act accordingly or relay it to sink/control center which might inform other actors.
(b) **Semi-Automated**
   The data acquired by sensors is relayed to sink/control center, which processes the data and issues respective commands to actors.

Figure 6 provides with an overview of WSAN architectures:

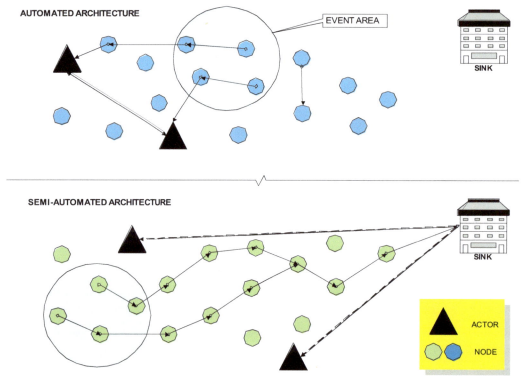

Fig. 6. Architecture Overview

The architecture selection entirely depends on the application requirements. Semi-Automated architecture is easy to implement because of its similarity to WSN applications [43], whereas Automated architecture offers advantages of *low latency* and *long network lifetime* with minimum hops and *resource saving* (energy, bandwidth), thus requires new protocols. These new protocols in addition to above characteristics should also address the sensor-actor and actor-actor coordination challenges as discussed in [44].

WSAN, still in its infancy offers added advantage of agents acting on our behalf. This new dimension has posed new challenges in terms of requirement of new algorithms and protocols but promises immense potential in terms of applications. With its applications encompassing all domains, two major applications are discussed below:

Search and Rescue Operation

Natural and human-induced disasters result in collapsed buildings with highest probability. Immediate and effective response is desired in such scenarios to minimize loss of lives. Unfortunately, such search and rescue operations are highly sensitive and slow paced, as heavy machinery would risk life of rescuers and survivors, entailing manual and by hand removal of debris. Search and rescue operation to-date still relies on old technologies such as search dogs, camera mounted probes, and technology that has been in service for decades. These methodologies help in detecting survivor but are unable to provide description of the physical environment the victim locates, even camera mounted probes have effective range no more than 4-6 meters along a straight line below ground surface [45].

Fig. 7. Pakistan earthquake 2005, a collapsed girl's college. (Courtesy of Dr. Albert Ko, University of Hong Kong) [45]

Robots have been designed for such operations [46], but they have been restricted to literature with no significant demonstration till 2001.These robots can navigate successfully through the rubble and look for survivors but localization is important as soon as they get out of sight.

A WSAN with mobile robots as actors can provide a perfect solution for search and rescue operations. Nodes scattered around the target area in the form of clusters can help localize the actors for successful navigation into rubble using localization techniques based on radio range measurements, like Time of Arrival (ToA) or Radio Signal Strength (RSS) methods. This makes void the need of other localization methods such as GPS which is not feasible for dense areas especially inside buildings because of low resolution, whereas WSAN can provide precision in range of centimeters with increased nodal density at low costs. Therefore, WSAN search and rescue team forms a truly applicable system with no set up time for emergency operations.

Military Applications

WSAN, still at an early stage has immense prospects in military domain. These networks will directly influence and change the way military operates whether in peace or at war. With characteristics to localize, detect, rescue, evade, differentiate, pursue and coordinate etc, WSAN based actors (robots, UAV's etc) will replace soldiers in battle field for all sort of activities such as autonomous infiltration into enemy areas, target destruction, surveillance and active border patrolling against insurgents and terrorists, reconnoitering of unknown and hostile regions etc.

Such networks can be effectively employed during and after war for search and removal of landmines especially in war struck areas with civilian population, which unfortunately, to date are still scattered in countries like Vietnam, Cambodia and Afghanistan.

Other applications areas include home automation, environmental and habitat monitoring, agricultural monitoring and nuclear, chemical leakage detection etc to name a few.

CONCLUSION

Concept of global automation and actuation has emerged in the form of Wireless Sensor Networks. Developments in terms of operating systems, communication standards, microprocessors and MEMS sensors and transceivers have significantly influenced the WSN industry. Though these developments have miniaturized sensor nodes significantly, the true form of these nodes will exist in a single System on Chip (SOC) replacing a sensor node. In not so distant future, these nodes will not only be embedded but a part of our lives in form of smart bolts holding large structures, smart girders in building ensuring structure stability, instrumented in watches, teapots, bed etc helping our elders to live a comfortable life and everywhere possible from soil, sky and sea to our homes and gardens. This is the future of WSNs, becoming a proactive positive member of our ecosystem.

References

[1]   www.zigbee.org, [Accessed July. 15, 2009]
[2]   David C. Snowdon, Sergio Ruocco and Gernot Heiser, *"Power management and dynamic voltage scaling: Myths and facts"*, Proceedings of the 2005 Workshop on Power Aware Real-time Computing, New Jersey, USA, September, 2005.
[3]   Gang Qu, "What is the limit of energy saving by dynamic voltage scaling?", in IEEE/ACM international conference on computer-aided design, 2001, pp. 560 – 563.
[4]   Kazem Sohraby, Daniel Minoli and Taieb Znati, "Wireless sensor networks: technology, protocols, and applications", John Wiley & Sons, Inc, 2007.
[5]   Wouter Horré , Sam Michiels , Nelson Matthys , Wouter Joosen , Pierre Verbaeten, "On the integration of sensor networks and general purpose IT infrastructure", Proceedings of the 2nd international workshop on Middleware for sensor networks, 2007, p.7-12.
[6]   Adi Mallikarjuna Reddy V AVU Phani Kumar, D Janakiram, and G Ashok Kumar, "Wireless sensor network operating systems: a survey", International Journal of Sensor Networks 2009 - Vol. 5, No.4 pp. 236 - 255.
[7]   Donald Thompson, Colin Miller, "Introducing the .NET Micro Framework, Product Positioning and Technology White Paper",   September   7,   2007.   <   http://download.microsoft.com/download/a/   9/c/a9cb2192-8429-474a-aa56-534fffb5f0f1/.NET%20Micro%20 Framework%20White%20Paper.doc>. [Accessed July. 10, 2009].
[8]   B. Peters, ''Sensing Without wires: Wireless Sensing Solves Many Problems, But Introduces a Few of Its Own,'' Machine   Design,   Penton   Media,   Cleveland,   OH, <http://www.machinedesign.com/ASP/viewSelectedArticle.asp?strArticleId=57795&str-&strSite=MDSite&Screen =&CURRENTISSUE &CatID=3 >.
[9]   http://enaweb.eng.yale.edu/drupal/system/files/ CC2420_ Data_ Sheet_1_4.pdf. [Accessed July. 15, 2009]
[10]   http://www.atmel.com/dyn/resources/prod_documents/doc8111.pdf. [Accessed July. 15, 2009]

[11]   F.L. Lewis, Ed., D.J. Cook and S.K. Das, "Wireless Sensor Networks", in Smart Environments: Technologies, Protocols, Applications, New York: Wiley, 2004.

[12]   http://www.rfm.com/products/data/wsn802g.pdf. [Accessed July 15, 2009]

[13]   http://www.cirronet.com/07cdcatalog/print_catalog/802_industrial.pdf. [Accessed July. 15, 2009]

[14]   R. Siegwart, I. Nourbakhsh, "Introduction to autonomous mobile robots", MIT Press, 2004.

[15]   http://www.engineershandbook.com/Components/sensors.htm. [Accessed July. 10, 2009]

[16]   M. Minami, T. Morito, H. Morikawa, and T. Aoyama. Solar biscuit, "A battery-less wireless sensor network system for environmental monitoring applications". in 2nd International Workshop on Networked Sensing Systems, 2005.

[17]   Doru E. Tiliute, "Battery Management in Wireless Sensor Networks", Electronics and Electrical Engineering Journal, Nr. 4(76) / 2007.

[18]   M. Halpern and K. Saleem, Battery Power Issues for WSN's, slideshow presented at NICTA Workshop on Formal Methods for Wireless Networks, Sydney, 2005. < http://www.cse.unsw.edu.au/~formalmethods/events/fmwsn-05/Saleem-Halpern.ppt >. [Accessed July. 10, 2009].

[19]   Raghunathan V, "Design Considerations for Solar Energy Harvesting Wireless Embedded Systems" // IPSN 2005. in fourth International Symposium on Information Processing in Sensor Networks, 2005. pp. 457–462.

[20]   Chulsung Park, Jinfeng Liu, Pai H. Chou, "Eco: An Ultra-Compact Low-Power Wireless Sensor Node for Real-Time Motion Monitoring", in Fourth International Symposium on Information Processing in Sensor Networks, 2005, pp. 398-403

[21]   http://www.xbow.com/Products/Product_pdf_files/Wireless_pdf/Imote2_Datasheet.pdf. [Accessed July. 13, 2009]

[22]   http://www.xbow.com/Products/Product_pdf_files/Wireless_pdf/MICA2_Datasheet.pdf. [Accessed July. 13, 2009]

[23]   http://www.xbow.com/Products/Product_pdf_files/Wireless_pdf/TelosB_Datasheet.pdf. [Accessed July. 13, 2009]

[24]   http://www.csiro.org/resources/Smart-Sensor-Network-Technology.html. [Accessed July 13, 2009]

[25]   Ross P.E., "Managing Care through the Air" IEEE Spectrum, Dec 2004; pp. 14-19.

[26]   Benny Lo, Surapa Thiemjarus, Rachel King and Guang Zhong Yang, "Body Sensor Network A Wireless Sensor Platform for Pervasive Healthcare Monitoring", Adjunct Proceedings of the 3rd International Conference on Pervasive Computing (PERVASIVE 2005), May 2005, pp.77-80.

[27]   J. P. Lynch and K. J. Loh, "A Summary Review of Wireless Sensors and Sensor Networks for Structural Health Monitoring", in Shock and Vibration Digest, Sage 2006, pp. 91-128.

[28]   Farrar, C. R., "Historical Overview of Structural Health Monitoring", Lecture Notes on Structural Health Monitoring Using Statistical Pattern Recognition, Los Alamos Dynamics, Los Alamos, NM, 2001.

[29]   Binns, J. "Bridge Sensor System Delivers Results Quickly", Civil Engineering, 2004 Vol. 74, No. 9, pp. 30–31.

[30]   Farhey, D. N., "Rapid-response Diagnostics and Smart Structure Monitoring in Bridge Testing", in Proceedings of the County Engineers Association of Ohio Bridge Conference, Columbus, OH, 2003.

[31]   Österlind, Fredrik and Pramsten, Erik and Roberthson, Daniel and Eriksson, Joakim and Finne, Niclas and Voigt, Thiemo "Integrating Building Automation Systems and Wireless Sensor Networks." in 12th IEEE Conference on Emerging Technologies and Factory Automation, 25-28 September 2007, pp. 1376 – 1379.

[32]   Waltenegus Dargie and Marco Zimmerling, "Wireless Sensor Networks in the Context of Developing Countries (invited paper)." The 3rd IFIP World Information Technology Forum (WITFOR). Addis Ababa, Ethiopia, August 22-24, 2007.

[33]   G. Werner-Allen, K. Lorincz, M. Welsh, O. Marcillo, J. Johnson, M. Ruiz, and J. Lees, "Deploying a wireless sensor network on an active volcano", IEEE Internet Computing, vol. 10, Mar. 2006, pp. 18-25.

[34]   A.-S. K. Pathan, C. S. Hong, and H.-W. Lee, "Smartening the environment using wireless sensor networks in a developing country", in Proc. IEEE International Workshop on Advanced Communication Technology (ICACT 2006), Feb. 2006, pp. 705–709.

[35]   A. Mainwaring, D. Culler, J. Polastre, R. Szewczyk and J. Anderson, "Wireless Sensor Networks for Habitat Monitoring", in Proceedings of the First ACM International Workshop on Wireless Sensor Networks and Applications (WSNA 02), Georgia, September 2002, pp. 88 – 97.

[36]   www.ee.princeton.edu/~mrm/zebranet.html. [Accessed July. 7, 2009]

[37]   http://www.wfp.org/hunger. [Accessed July. 25, 2009]

[38]   A. Baggio, "Wireless Sensor Networks in Precision Agriculture," Proc. ACM Workshop Real-World Wireless Sensor Networks, 2005.

[39]   Chibuzor Edordu and Lionel Sacks, "Self Organising Wireless Sensor Networks as a Land Management Tool in Developing Countries: A Preliminary Survey", London Communications Symposium (LCS), 2006.

[40]   R. Beckwith, D. Teibel, and P. Bowen, "Unwired wine: sensor networks in vineyards", 2004, pp. 561-564.

[41]   I. F. Akyildiz, T. Melodia, and K. R. Chowdury, "Wireless Multimedia Sensor Networks: Applications and Testbeds," in Proceedings of the IEEE, Vol. 96, No. 10. (2008), pp. 1588-1605.

[42]   I. F. Akyildiz, T. Melodia, and K. R. Chowdhury, "A survey on wireless multimedia sensor networks", Computer Networks. (Elsevier), vol. 51, no. 4, Mar. 2007, pp. 921–960.

[43]   I.F. Akyildiz, W. Su, Y. Sankarasubramaniam, E. Cayirci, "Wireless sensor networks: A survey", Computer Networks 38 (4) 2002, pp. 393–422.

[44]   I. F. Akyildiz and I. H. Kasimoglu,"Wireless Sensor and Actor Networks: Research Challenges," Ad Hoc Networks Journal (Elsevier), Vol. 2, No. 4, October 2004, pp. 351-367.

[45]   Albert Ko and Henry Y. K. Lau, "Robot Assisted Emergency Search and Rescue System With a Wireless Sensor Network", International Journal of Advanced Science and Technology, Vol. 3, February 2009.

[46]   Kobayashi, A. and Nakamura, K. "Rescue Robot for Fire Hazards", Proc. of International Conference on Advanced Robotics, 1983, pp 91-98.

CHAPTER 5

Ultra Wideband Wireless Sensor Networks

S. Mehta and K.S. Kwak

UWB Wireless Communications Research Center, Inha University, Korea.

Abstract: Ultra-Wideband (UWB) has recently gained great interest for high-speed short-range communications (e.g. Wireless Sensor Networks/home networking applications) as well as low-speed long-range communications as it can offer unique advantages for wireless communications such as precise location-timing capabilities, imperceptibility, low power, low complexity, and low cost. In this chapter, we present an overview of UWB system and a performance analysis of UWB based MAC protocol of high data rate, short range communication, especially, on the IEEE 802.15.3 MAC protocol for wireless sensor networks. We use analytical model to present some illustrative channel capacity results, and provide a discussion of the impact of various acknowledgment schemes on multiple access capacity under different parameters. Also, some important observations are obtained, which can be very useful to UWB MAC protocol architectures as well as to UWB application designers. Finally, we present some important research issues and challenges to further investigate the possible improvements in the UWB system.

INTRODUCTION

Ultra-Wideband (UWB) as a technology has been around since 1970s but was primarily used in the military for radar based applications. UWB communication has been synonymous with "impulse radio" for a long time. Recently, UWB has gained great interest for high speed short range communication as well as low speed long range communication. The FCC defines a signal to be ultra-wideband if its fractional bandwidth is greater than 20 % or the bandwidth occupies 500 MHz or more of the spectrum. An example comparison of narrowband (NB), spread spectrum (SS), and ultra-wideband (UWB) bandwidth concepts is shown in figure 1.

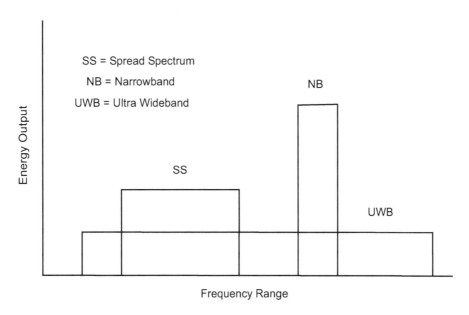

Fig. 1. Comparison of narrowband, spread spectrum, and Ultra-Wideband

As shown in figure 1, UWB signals occupy several octaves of frequency spectrum they are likely to interfere with other narrow band systems. Hence, UWB signals have to operate with very low transmit power. Some of the potential advantages of using UWB signals are [1]:

∞Capability of co-existence with other narrowband and UWB systems
∞Security
∞Immunity from multi-path
∞Simple to integrate on chip

Along with all the aforementioned advantages there are several practical issues need to be solved to open the potential gate of UBW technology. These practical challenges includes Multi-access code design, multiple access interference (MAI) cancellation, synchronization of the receiver to extremely narrow pulses, accurate modeling of UWB channels, estimation of multipath channel delays and coefficients, to name a few [1, 2]. Moreover, the UWB technology in wireless networks is still at the nascent stage as there is a wide range of questions open to further investigation in addition to the aforementioned physical layer/practical issues.

APPLICATIONS

UWB has several applications all the way from wireless communications to radar imaging, and vehicular radar. UWB has been targeted to serve two basic spheres of wireless communication.

High data rate and low range communication: UWB technology is a potential candidate to provide high data rate up to 1 Gbps especially for indoor applications. Because of this high data rate capability UWB can bee seen as an alternative to Bluetooth technology. One of the potential applications is Wireless Personal Area Networks (WPAN) based home entertaining application. In this application all the nodes (i.e. digital devices) such as DVD player, HDTV, surround sound speakers, etc., can be connected wirelessly to each other, and they can also form their own home network. It is also possible to integrate Wireless LAN/Ethernet to this "home" network. With this home network, we can link multiple TVs in different room to receive the same multimedia content, and similar many more multimedia applications are also possible. One more important application is in the battlefield to provide a high data rate, high speed, and secure data communication. UWB is also being considered for wireless sensor/Ad-hoc networks, especially for high-data-rate applications such as body area networks, WPAN, etc., [2, 3].

Low data rate and long range communication: There are several applications where UWB technology can be used for larger range and low data rate applications. Typical examples include, habitat monitoring wireless sensor networks, tactical communications, and intrusion detection radars. UWB is one of the potential candidates for physical layer technology in wireless sensor networks due to its low transmits power requirements. Although there are many long range applications in UWB technology, lots of research efforts are made for short range, high data rate applications as it has huge commercial possibilities. In this chapter, we also focus on high data rate and short range communication aspect of UBW.

Having discussed the advantages and the applications of the technology we can now draw our attention into the functionality and MAC layer designs for the UWB system. The main goal of the MAC layer is to allow the number of users to share a common medium. Beside channel access mechanism MAC layer also includes marinating quality of service, power management, mobility management and security. Existing wireless MAC layer protocols are not suitable or optimized for the UWB system due to unique characteristics of UWB technology. So, an UWB based system MAC layer needs special design considerations such as high channel time acquisition time ranging abilities, low power operation, carrier less pulse position modulation, and interoperability between exiting narrow band technologies and UWB technology.

In this chapter, we mainly focus on designing and analysis of UWB based MAC protocol of high data rate, short range communication, especially, on the IEEE 802.15.3 MAC protocol for wireless sensor networks. We use analytical model to study the performance analysis of IEEE 802.15.3 MAC in terms of throughput, efficient bandwidth utilization, and delay with various acknowledgment schemes under different parameters. Also, some important observations are obtained, which can be very useful to the protocol architectures as well as to UWB sensor networks application designers.

The rest of the chapter is organized as follows. High data rate UWB MAC protocol is presented in section 1.2. In section 1.3, we present UWB MAC Protocol Designing and performance analysis from protocol architecture's point of view. Finally, future research directions and summary are drawn in section 1.4 and 1.5, respectively.

HIGH DATA RATE UWB MAC PROTOCOL: IEEE 802.15.3

Nowadays the UWB technique is a promising candidate in the development of WPANs. The IEEE 802.15.3a task group has been working towards amending the 802.15.3 standard to serve as the MAC/PHY standard for UWB WPANs [4]. However, the high data rate PHY layer extension for IEEE 802.15.3, IEEE 802.15.3a, has not been finalized so far and moreover, some issues of the high data rate UWB system to existing systems are not solved yet [5-7].

The IEEE standard 802.15.3 MAC layer [8] is based on a centralized, connection oriented topology which divides a large network into several smaller ones termed "piconets". As shown in figure 2, a piconet consists of a Piconet Network Controller (PNC) and DEVs (DEVices). The DEV is designed to be low power and low cost. One DEV is required to perform the role of PNC (Piconet Coordinator), which provides the basic timing for the piconet as well as other piconet management functions, such as power management, Quality of Service (QoS) scheduling, and security,.

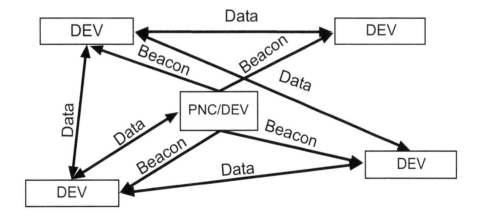

Fig. 2. Piconet Structure in IEEE 802.15.3

Using the formation of child and neighboring piconets user can increase the range of network span. The WPAN starter piconet is called as "parent piconet" and child/neighbor piconets are called "dependent piconets". These piconets differ in the way they associate themselves to the parent piconet. The specific functionalities of IEEE 802.15.3 will be described in brief in the following sections. In short, the design goals of IEEE 802.15.3 MAC protocol are as follows:

∞Fast connection
∞Ad-hoc networks
∞Data transport with quality of service (QoS)
∞Security
∞Dynamic membership
∞Efficient data transfer

IEEE 802.15.3 standard supports multiple power saving modes and multiple acknowledgement (ACK) policies (NO ACK, Imm-ACK, Del-ACK, and Implied-ACK) [8]. It is very robust and supports coexistence with the other WLAN technologies such as IEEE 802.11. In IEEE 802.15.3 MAC protocol, at first connection and initial communication are established by PNC later nodes can transfer the data in peer to peer manner. In IEEE 802.15.3 MAC protocol, time is divided into many superframes and every superframe into three parts: the beacon, the optional contention access period (CAP), and the channel time allocation period (CTAP) or channel time allocation time (CTA), as shown in figure 3. The maximum length of a super-frame is 65.536 msec.

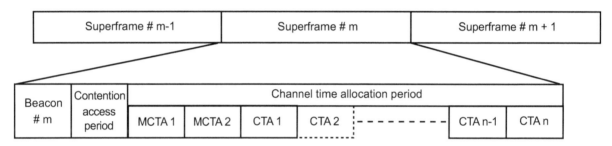

Fig. 3. Superframe structure of IEEE 802.15.3 MAC

Beacon: All the nodes in a piconet synchronize to the PNC clock at the beginning of the beacon preamble. The PNC controls the type of data or commands that may be sent in the CAP or CFP period via the different control bits in the beacon frame. So basically beacon is used to transmit control information, the allocated channel time allocation (CTA) for the current superframe and to provide network wide timing information.

Contention Access Period (CAP): This part is similar to distributed coordination function (DCF) of IEEE 802.11. Any node can send its asynchronous data during this time. The time period is also used for channel time requests, authentication, association request/response, asynchronous data, and other commands in the system. Communication during this part of the frame uses the CSMA/CA protocol with back-off procedure similar to IEEE 802.11 DCF.

Contention Free Period (CFP) or Channel time Allocations (CTA): This part is similar to TDMA based MAC protocol where each slot is assigned to a particular pair of nodes. This is very important to support real time video/audio applications as they have very stringent requirements on timing jitter, end-to-end delay etc. CFP is further divided into two parts: channel time allocation (CTA) and Management Time Slot (MTS). To get a slot(s) in CFP cycle each node makes a channel time request during the CAP. Then PNC node declares the assignments of CTA/MTS to other nodes during the beacon time.

DATA COMMUNICATION IN A PICONET

In this section we briefly described the communication procedure in a piconet. As shown in figure 2 all the data in a piconet is exchanged in peer to peer manner. At the start PNC node transmits the beacon at the start of every superframe. If any node wants to communicate with destination node, it transmits the channel time request (CTRq) to PNC during the CAP time with all the information (i.e. source ID, destination ID, etc.). Then PNC node sends the Channel Time Response (CTRp) to indicate the responding CTA information to the requesting node. PNC node should allocate different slots in CFP for different pair of nodes. All the slots and its occupancy information for current superframe are broadcast in the beacon. According to this information the source node adjusts its transmission cycle, power level, and transmission rate for reliable communications. Every node in piconet follows its own transmission schedules, hence no interference exists, and a reliable communication is guaranteed [8].

Acknowledgement Schemes:

Wireless channel is usually vulnerable to errors. Hence, error control mechanism is an essential part of any MAC protocol design. A good error control mechanism provides a certain level of reliability in terms of communication robustness and dependability for higher network layers. In accordance with that, IEEE 802.15.3 standard defines three types of acknowledgment mechanisms for CTAs and CAPs as follow:

No-ACK: In No-ACK (No-Acknowledgement) mechanism, ACK is not sent after a reception of message. This mechanism is useful for only high data rate applications where guaranteed delivery is not required or acknowledgement is handled by higher layers or by some other mechanism.

Imm-ACK: In Imm-ACK (Immediate Acknowledgement), mechanism, each received data frame is individually acknowledged after the successful reception. This mechanism gives more simple and stable operation compared to No-ACK but at the cost of reduced data rate.

Dly-ACK: In Dly-ACK (delay-acknowledgement) mechanism, receiver sent an acknowledge frame for a group of data frames rather than an individual data frame. This mechanism is a tradeoff between No-ACK and Imm-ACK. Both Imm-ACK and Dly-ACK have adopted retransmission method to recover the corrupted frames in unsuccessful transmissions [9].

In [8] and some other literature proposed implied-acknowledgment (Imp-ACK) for bidirectional communication. Implied acknowledgement (Imp-ACK) permits a CTA to be used bi-directionally within a limited scope. During the CAP, Imp-ACK is not allowed to avoid ambiguities between two frames; (a) the frame that is transmitted in response to a frame with an implied ACK request, and (b) the frame that is transmitted independently when the original frame is unsuccessfully received. In this paper we focused only on the three aforementioned acknowledgement schemes as Imp-ACK is neither widely accepted in research literature nor in standard documents. Figure 4 shows different ACK policies in IEEE 802.15.3 [10].

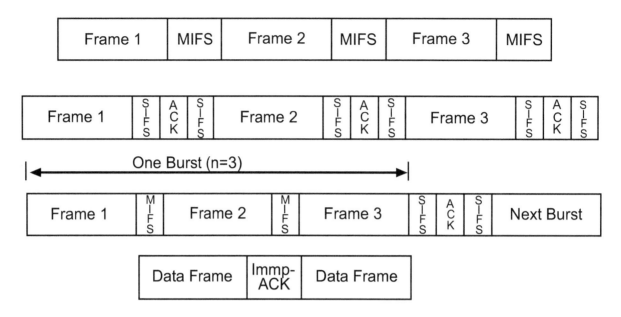

Fig. 4. NO-ACK, Imm-ACK,Dly-ACK (burst Size=3), and Implied-ACK: Different ACK policies in the IEEE 802.15.3

To reduce the overhead of the IEEE 802.15.3 MAC, we use the concept of frame aggregation .The idea of frame aggregation is to aggregate multiple MAC frames into a single (or approximately single) transmission [11]. In this chapter we combine the frame aggregation concept and Dly-ACK mechanism with minor modification and we define this new mechanism as K-Dly-ACK-AGG, where K is the burst size of data frames, [12]. Imm-ACK with aggregation method act same as K-Dly-ACK-AGG (Where $K=1$) so there is no point to consider Imm-ACK policy individually with aggregation.

All these ACK policies have a large impact on the throughput, delay, and channel utilization of the network and required a detailed study to find overall performance or channel capacity of the network. In this paper, we present the performance analysis of IEEE 802.15.3 from protocol architecture's point of view. Furthermore, we show the effect of aggregation with Dly-ACK,i.e., K-Dly-ACK-AGG, on the network performance.

Power Management in IEEE 802.15.3:

As IEEE 802.15.3 is specially used for wireless sensor networks, it is very important goal of IEEE 802.15.3 to introduce some power saving modes. In this regard IEEE 802.15.3 MAC support three power saving modes: device synchronized power save (DSPS) mode, piconet synchronized power save (PSPS) mode, and asynchronous power save (APS) mode. Every node has two states:Awake and Sleep, in any given power saving mode. During the sleep time the node switch off its radio and switch on during the awake time.

PSPS Mode: In this mode all nodes can sleep at intervals defined by the PNC. In this mode a node is required to listen to all system wakeup beacons and be in the awake state during the system wakeup superframes.

DSPS Mode: This mode is designed to enable groups of nodes (i.e. a set of nodes) to sleep for multiple superframes. Nodes can synchronize their sleeping pattern by joining a DSPS mode enable 'set'. The main drawback of PSPS and DSPS modes is that they are not efficient for multimedia traffic which is non-periodic in nature.

APS Mode: This mode is specially designed for non-periodic traffics. In APS mode, a node has to communicate with the PNC before the end of its association timeout period (ATP) to maintain its association with the piconet. However, when a node sleep for longer time than ATP, this mode increases the overhead to maintain the association and that results in increased power consumption. For more details on the power saving modes readers are advised to refer [8].

Ad-Hoc Networking Using IEEE 802.15.3:

Generally, a piconet's range is defined for few meters so multi-hop communication is must to increase the coverage of IEEE 802.15.3 network. As we discussed earlier, designer can use the formation of child and neighboring piconets for the same. The WPAN starter piconet is called as "parent piconet" and child/neighbor piconets are called "dependent piconets". These piconets differ in the way they associate themselves to the parent piconet.

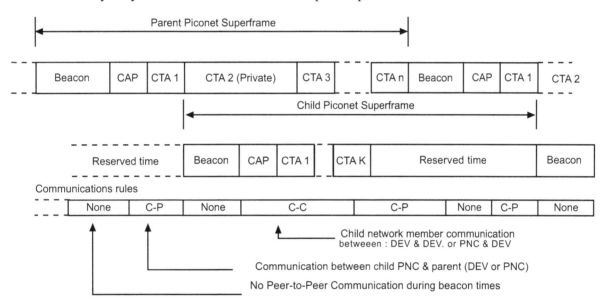

Fig. 5(a). Superframe structure of parent piconet and child piconet

Generally, the child piconet is used for extending the range while the neighbor piconet is used for sharing the same frequency spectrum between different piconets. From figure 5, we can see the superframe relationship of parent piconet and child piconet as well as the parent piconet and neighbor piconet. The difference between figure 5(a) and 5(b) is self explained. In parent piconet a private CTA time slot is used for a dependent piconet or other use. During the private CTA time slot, there are no transmissions from the parent piconets as it will interfere with the dependant piconet communication. As a result, the spectrum efficiency and throughput are low for the network. However, the bridging device between two piconets can improve the network performance. The bridging node is the device that belongs to two or more piconets simultaneously. And there are several issues need to be addressed in IEEE 802.15.3 based ad-hoc network designing as follows [8].

∞Piconet formation
∞Interpiconet scheduling
∞Joint scheduling and routing
∞Latency reduction in route discovery and rediscovery
∞Piconet-aware routing scheme etc.

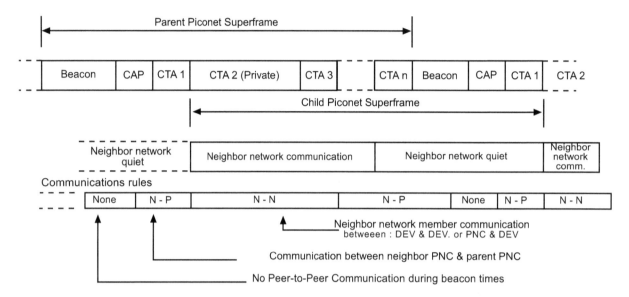

Fig. 5(b). Superframe structure of parent piconet and neighbor piconet

UWB MAC PROTOCOL DESIGNING AND ANALYSIS

To the best of our knowledge, there is little work on the performance or channel analysis of IEEE 802.15.3 MAC with respect to different ACK policies, under different parameters. However, a large amount of literature is available on IEEE 802.15.3 MAC scheduling, optimization of superframe size, and various traffic analyses. Some of the important related works are as follow. In [5] authors, presents the implementation of IEEE 802.15.3 module in ns-2 and discuses various experimental scenario results including various scheduling techniques. Specially, to investigate the performance of real-time and best-effort traffic with various super frame lengths and different ACK policies. In [10, 14], the authors presents an adaptive Dly-ACK scheme for both TCP and UDP traffic. The first one is to request the Dly-ACK frame adaptively or change the burst size of Dly-ACK according to the transmitter queue status. The second is a retransmission counter to enable the destination DEV to deliver the MAC data frames to upper layer timely and orderly. While later is more focused on optimization of channel capacity. Both papers laid a good foundation in simulation and analytical works of IEEE 802.15.3 MAC protocol. Similarly, in [9] authors, formulate a throughput optimization problem under error channel condition and derive a closed form solution for the optimal throughput. The work presents in [9] is close to our work but their analysis scope is limited only in terms of throughput analysis. While our work span covers the delay, throughput, and channel utilization with different ACK policies under frame aggregation and error channel condition.

Performance Analysis of IEEE 802.15.3 MAC Protocol:

In this section, we present the designing and analysis of IEEE 802.15.3 MAC to answer several questions like optimization of payload, optimization of ACK policies, and effect of aggregation, under various parameters.

Analytical Model:

We use ground works of Bianchis's model [15] and [9] to present our analysis work. Table 1 shows the notations that we used for the analytical model.

Table I. Parameters notations

T_{SIFS}	Short Inter Frame Space (SIFS) time
T_{DIFS}	Distributed Coordinate Function Inter Frame Space (DIFS) time
T_{MIFS}	Minimum Inter Frame Space (MIFS) time
CW_{min}	Minimum back-off window size
$T_{pre.}$	Transmission time of the physical preamble
T_{PHY}	Transmission time of the PHY header
L_{MAC-H}	MAC overhead in bytes
L_{ACK}	ACK size in bytes
L_{Data}	Payload size in bytes
T_{MAC-H}	Transmission time of MAC overhead
T_{Data}	Transmission time for the payload
L_{MAC-HS}	MAC Sub-header bytes
T_{f-CAP}	The time for a transmission considered failed during CAP
T_{s-CAP}	The time for a transmission considered successful during CAP
T_{f-CTA}	The time for a transmission considered failed during CAT
T_{s-CTA}	The time for a transmission considered successful during CAT
T_{ACK-TO}	The time-out value waiting for an ACK
Th_{CAP}	Normalized throughput during a CAP time
Th_{CTA}	Normalized throughput during a CTA time
K	Burst size in packets

The theoretical throughput is given by

$$Th = \frac{Transmitted\ Data}{Transmission\ Cycle\ Duration} \qquad (1)$$

We assume a Gaussian wireless channel model. Although the Gaussian channel model cannot capture the multi-path fading characteristics of a wireless channel, it is widely used because of its simplicity. The channel bit error rate (BER), denoted as p_e $(0 < p_e < 1)$, can be calculated via previous frames or some other mechanism. How to obtain p_e is way out of the scope of this paper. From [15], a frame with a length L in bits, the probability that the frame is successfully transmitted can be calculated as

$$p_s = (1 - p_e)^L \qquad (2)$$

Here, for the simplicity we assume that a data frame is considered to be successfully transmitted if both data frame and ACK are successfully transmitted in different ACK mechanism policies. We use Imm-ACK, No-ACK, Dly-ACK, and K-Dly-AGG-ACK to denote the immediate acknowledgement, No acknowledgement, delay acknowledgement, and delay acknowledgement with aggregation, respectively. Then we can define p_s for different ACK mechanisms as follows

$$p_s, \text{Imm-ACK} = (1 - p_e)^{(L_{Data} + L_{MAC-H} + L_{ACK-Imm})*8}$$
$$p_s, \text{No-ACK} = (1 - p_e)^{(L_{Data} + L_{MAC-H})*8}$$
$$p_s, \text{Dly-ACK} = (1 - p_e)^{(L_{Data} + L_{MAC-H} + L_{ACK-Dly})K*8} \qquad (3)$$
$$p_s, \text{Dly-ACK-AGG} = (1 - p_e)^{(L_{Data} + L_{MAC-H} + L_{MAC-Hs} + L_{ACK-Dly})K*8}$$

A successful transmission time during a CTA is given by

$$T_{s-CTA} = \begin{cases} \left(T_{SIFS} + T_{Data} + T_{MAC-H} + T_{pre} + T_{PHY}\right) & \text{for No - ACK} \\ \left(2*T_{SIFS} + T_{Data} + T_{MAC-H} + 2*T_{pre} + T_{PHY} + T_{MAC-ACK} + T_{PHY-ACK} + T_{Imm-ACK}\right) & \text{for Imm - ACK} \\ \left(K(T_{SIFS} + T_{Data} + T_{MAC-H} + T_{pre} + T_{PHY}) + T_{SIFS} + T_{MAC-ACK} + T_{PHY-ACK} + T_{Dly-ACK} + T_{pre}\right) & \text{for Dly - ACK} \\ \left(K*T_{Data} + T_{MAC-H} + T_{MAC-HS} + 2*T_{pre} + T_{PHY} + T_{SIFS} + T_{MAC-ACK} + T_{PHY-ACK} + T_{Dly-ACK-AGG}\right) & \text{for Dly - ACK - AGG} \end{cases} \qquad (4)$$

from (2), (3) and (4) the throughput during a CTA is given by

$$Th_{CTA} = \begin{cases} \dfrac{p_s, No-ACK L_{Data}*8}{T_{s-CTA}} & \text{for No - ACK} \\ \dfrac{p_s, Imm-ACK L_{Data}*8}{T_{s-CTA}} & \text{for Imm - ACK} \\ \dfrac{p_s, Dly-ACK K L_{Data}*8}{T_{s-CTA}} & \text{for Dly - ACK} \\ \dfrac{p_s, Dly-ACK-AGG K L_{Data}*8}{T_{s-CTA}} & \text{for Dly - ACK - AGG} \end{cases} \qquad (5)$$

Based on the analytical model presented in [16], the upper theoretical throughput limit during a CTA is given by

$$Th_{UL-CTA} = \begin{cases} \dfrac{KL_{Data}*8}{2*T_{PHY}+2*T_{pre}+T_{MIFS}+T_{DIFS}} & for\ ACK-AGG \\[2ex] \dfrac{L_{Data}*8}{T_{PHY}+T_{pre}+T_{MIFS}+T_{DIFS}} & for\ No-ACK \\[2ex] \dfrac{KL_{Data}*8}{T_{PHY}+T_{pre}+T_{MIFS}+T_{DIFS}} & for\ No-ACK-AGG \end{cases} \quad (6)$$

To demonstrate the effect of *K*-Dly-ACK and *K*-Dly-ACK-AGG on bandwidth utilization, we define a metric named maximum effective bandwidth (MEB) based on [17], which is a fraction of time the channel is used to successfully transmit data frames versus the total channel time. The maximum effective bandwidth utilization during a CTA/CAP slot is given by

$$MEB_{CTA} = \begin{cases} K.\dfrac{L_{Data}p_s,Dly-ACK}{T_{s-CTA}} & for\ Dly-ACK \\[2ex] K.\dfrac{L_{Data}p_s,Dly-ACK-AGG}{T_{s-CTA}} & for\ Dly-ACK-AGG \end{cases} \qquad MEB_{CAP} = \begin{cases} K.\dfrac{L_{Data}n\psi(1-\psi)^{n-1}p_s,Dly\text{-}ACK,}{T_{s-CAP}} & for\ Dly-ACK \\[2ex] K.\dfrac{L_{Data}n\psi(1-\psi)^{n-1}p_s,Dly-ACK-AGG}{T_{s-CAP}} & for\ Dly-ACK-AGG \end{cases} \quad (7)$$

Here, we study how to optimize the channel throughput using different ACK policies under error channel condition. During CAP, if Imm-ACK mechanism is used, every node acquires CSMA/CA with binary exponential backoff. During NO-ACK mechanism every node start with some fixed backoff window value without any knowledge of success/failure of transmitted data frames. When Dly-ACK mechanism is used, a node will randomly select some back of window value and send a number (*K*) of data frames each separated by an MIFS and a delay-request frame separated by an MIFS (as shown in fig. 3) once its backoff timer reaches zero, and will wait for an ACK. If a burst transmission of *K* data frames is assumed to be successful, then the sender will reset the backoff window to the initial value; otherwise, the backoff window will be doubled. *K*-Dly-ACK-AGG follows the same backoff procedure as Dly-ACK. From [15], the failure probability of a transmission during a CAP is given by

$$p_f = \begin{cases} 1-(1-p)p_s,Imm-ACK & for\ Imm-ACK \\ 1-(1-p)p_s,Dly-ACK, & for\ Dly-ACK \\ 1-(1-p)p_s,Dly-ACK-AGG, & for\ Dly-ACK-AGG \end{cases} \quad (8)$$

For *n* number of stations, the probability of a transmitted frame collision is given by

$$p = 1-(1-\psi)^{n-1} \qquad (9)$$

ψ, probability of a station to transmit during a generic (i.e., randomly chosen) slot time is also depends on number of retry limit. Then, the probability of the busy channel is given by

$$p_b = 1-(1-\psi)^n \qquad (10)$$

From (9) and (10), the probability of a successful transmission occurs in a slot time is given by

$$p_S = \begin{cases} n\psi(1-\psi)^{n-1}p_s, No-ACK, & for\ No-ACK \\ n\psi(1-\psi)^{n-1}p_s, Imm-ACK, & for\ Imm-ACK \\ n\psi(1-\psi)^{n-1}p_s, Dly-ACK, & for\ Dly-ACK \\ n\psi(1-\psi)^{n-1}p_s, Dly-ACK-AGG, & for\ Dly-ACK-AGG \end{cases} \quad (11)$$

A successful transmission time during a CAP is given by

$$T_{s-CAP} = \begin{cases} \left(\overline{CW}+T_{SIFS}+T_{Data}+T_{MAC-H}+T_{pre}+T_{PHY}\right) & for\ No-ACK \\ \left(\overline{CW}+2*T_{SIFS}+T_{Data}+T_{MAC-H}+2*T_{pre}+T_{PHY}+T_{MAC-ACK}+T_{PHY-ACK}+T_{Imm-ACK}\right) & for\ Imm-ACK \\ \left(\overline{CW}+K(T_{SIFS}+T_{Data}+T_{MAC-H}+T_{pre}+T_{PHY})+T_{SIFS}+T_{MAC-ACK}+T_{PHY-ACK}+T_{Dly-ACK}+T_{pre}\right) & for\ Dly-ACK \\ \left(\overline{CW}+K*T_{Data}+T_{MAC-H}+T_{MAC-HS}+2*T_{pre}+T_{PHY}+T_{SIFS}+T_{MAC-ACK}+T_{PHY-ACK}+T_{Dly-ACK-AGG}\right) & for\ Dly-ACK-AGG \end{cases} \quad (12)$$

where $\overline{CW}$ represents the average back-off time. The average back-off defines the back-off duration for "light loaded networks", i.e. when each station has access to the channel after the first back-off attempt and is given by

$$\overline{CW} = \frac{CW_{\min}.T_{slot}}{2} \quad (13)$$

A failure transmission time during a CTA is given by

$$T_{f-CTA} = \begin{cases} \left(T_{SIFS}+T_{Data}+T_{MAC-H}+T_{pre}+T_{PHY}\right) & for\ No-ACK \\ \left(T_{SIFS}+T_{Data}+T_{MAC-H}+T_{pre}+T_{PHY}+T_{ACK-To}\right) & for\ Imm-ACK \\ \left(K(T_{SIFS}+T_{Data}+T_{MAC-H}+T_{pre}+T_{PHY})+T_{ACK-To}+T_{SIFS}\right) & for\ Dly-ACK \\ \left(K*T_{Data}+T_{MAC-H}+T_{MAC-HS}+T_{pre}+T_{PHY}+T_{ACK-To}+T_{SIFS}\right) & for\ Dly-ACK-AGG \end{cases} \quad (14)$$

from (11), (12), and (14), the throughput during a CAP is given by

$$Th_{CAP} = \begin{cases} \dfrac{P_S L_{Data}*8}{(1-p_b)\delta+P_S T_{s-CAP}+(p_b-P_S)T_{f-CAP}} & for\ No-ACK \\[6pt] \dfrac{P_S L_{Data}*8}{(1-p_b)\delta+P_S T_{s-CAP}+(p_b-P_S)T_{f-CAP}} & for\ Imm-ACK \\[6pt] \dfrac{P_S K L_{Data}*8}{(1-p_b)\delta+P_S T_{s-CAP}+(p_b-P_S)T_{f-CAP}} & for\ Dly-ACK \\[6pt] \dfrac{P_S K L_{Data}*8}{(1-p_b)\delta+P_S T_{s-CAP}+(p_b-P_S)T_{f-CAP}} & for\ Dly-ACK-AGG \end{cases} \quad (15)$$

from [10], the upper theoretical throughput limit during a CAP is given by

$$Th_{UL-CAP} = \begin{cases} \dfrac{KL_{Data}*8}{\overline{CW}+2*T_{PHY}+2*T_{pre}+T_{MIFS}+T_{DIFS}} & for\ ACK-AGG \\[3mm] \dfrac{L_{Data}*8}{\overline{CW}+T_{PHY}+T_{pre}+T_{MIFS}+T_{DIFS}} & for\ No-ACK \\[3mm] \dfrac{KL_{Data}*8}{\overline{CW}+T_{PHY}+T_{pre}+T_{MIFS}+T_{DIFS}} & for\ No-ACK-AGG \end{cases} \qquad (16)$$

from (1), we can also calculate the average access delay during a CTA/CAP.

Performance Evaluation

For the performance evaluation, we adopt the following parameters from [18] as shown in table 2. For the analytical results we consider the UWB technology adopted at the Physical layer. Whenever necessary we choose the values of the physical layer dependent parameters by referring to [18]. Also, we didn't consider the scheduling algorithm used to allocate the channel time slots as it is outside the scope of this paper. The design of a simple but effective scheduling algorithm is still an open issue.

Table II. Parameters Values

Parameters	Values
SIFS	2.5 usec
MIFS	1 usec
Preamble and PLCP Header	9 usec
CW_{min}	8
Payload Size	1~5 KB
ACK Policy	3 basic +Dly-ACK-AGG policies
Data Rate	1~2 Gbps
Control Signal Rate	48 Mbps

CTA Analysis:

Figures 6 and 7 show the throughput for different payload sizes under a given BER value with different ACK polices with and without aggregation, respectively. Here, we can observe that No-ACK gives the superior results as most of the CTA time is utilized for data transfer. However, No-ACK policy is not suitable for every application and channel condition. The K-Dly-ACK-AGG1 policy can achieve somewhat close results to No-ACK policy, as it reduces the unnecessary inter-frame time as well as the header size. It can be seen that an optimal payload size exists for a given BER value. As shown in the mentioned figures the throughput first increases, and then decreases with increasing payload size (even with the aggregation) in error prone channels. This is because without the protection of FCS in individual payload frame, a single bit error may corrupt the whole frame which will waste lots of medium time usage and counteract the efficiency produced by an increased payload size. Figure 8 shows the normalized throughput for different BER values with different ACK policies when payload size is set to 1KB. As the BER value increases the throughput decreases. The No-ACK policy with aggregation has larger throughput over large range of BER values than any other ACK policies.

---

[1] In rest of the chapter we keep using terms "*K*-Dly-ACK-AGG" and "DLY-ACK with aggregation" interchangeably.

To find the effect of K-Dly-ACK on bandwidth utilization as well as to find the optimal value of burst size for K-Dly-ACK policy, we define the MEB metric in (6). Figures 9 and 10 show the MEB with different burst values under a given BER value. From these figures we can observe that burst size = 4 give good results in fairly all given payload values. Here, we define the access delay as the time from the moment a packet is ready to be transmitted to the moment the packet starts its successful transmission. For a WPAN designer it is very important to know the maximum possible delay limit for a given network. Figure 11 shows the access delay performance for different burst sizes with the aggregation method. Here, we only analyzed K-Dly-ACK-AGG policy to get the upper bound on the delay performance.

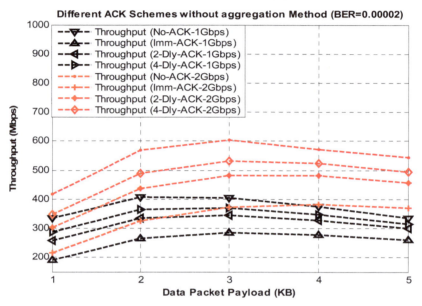

Fig. 6. Throughput versus payload size with different ACK policies

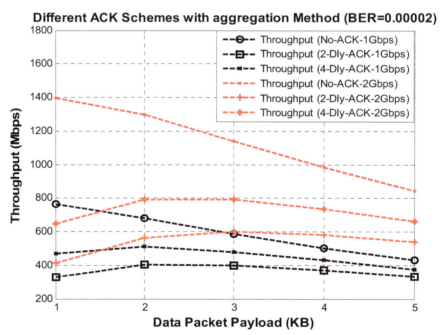

Fig. 7. Throughput versus payload size with different ACK policies

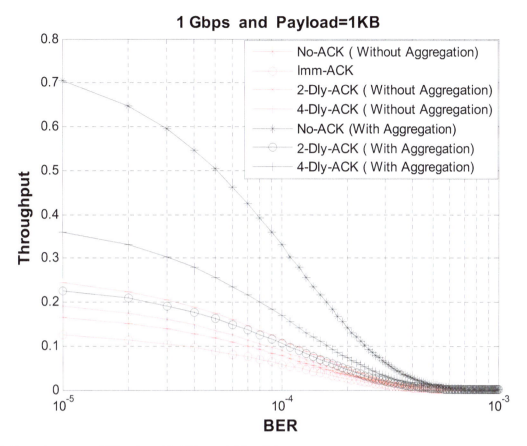

Fig. 8. Throughput versus BER value with Different ACK policies

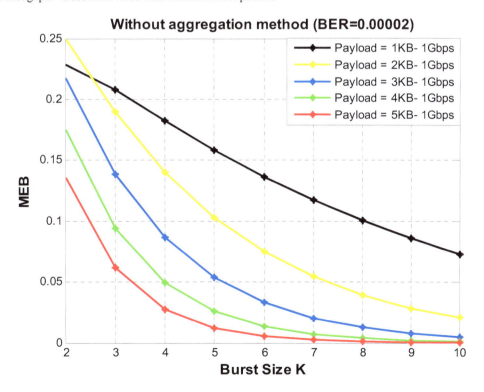

Fig. 9. MEB versus burst size

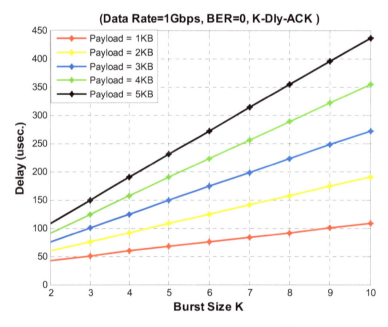

Fig. 10. MEB versus burst size

Fig. 11. Access delay versus burst size

CAP Analysis:

Figures 12 and 13 show the throughput for different payload sizes with different ACK policies under a given BER value. Here, we assume no competition between active nodes, as our main focus is to get maximum throughput for each payload size. For each ACK policies, with the increase of the payload size, the throughput first increases, then decreases after the maximal point. This can be explained as follows. In CAP, the time to transmit the payload is only a small portion of the total time used. Therefore, when the payload size increases, the transmission efficiency can be increase, but the error probability also increases. The increase of the curves in figures 12 and 13 is because the effect of increased transmission efficiency is more significant than the effect of increased frame error probability, and the decrease of the curves is due to dominant effect of increased frame error probability when payload size further increases. From the above mentioned figures we can find out the optimum payload size value for a given BER value. Here, it is worth to note that throughput performance depends on the number of active stations and backoff window size during a CAP time. Figure 14 shows the normalized throughput for different BER values when payload size is set to 1KB.

Similar to CTA analysis, Figure 15 and 16 shows the MEB for different burst values under a given BER value. Figure 17 shows the access delay performance for different burst sizes under a given BER value. The access delay performance with different ACK policies is very sensitive to backoff window size and number of active nodes. The K-Dly-ACK-AGG policy gives the upper bound on the delay performance.

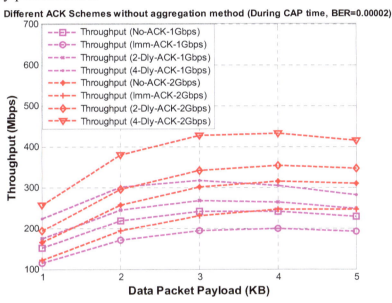

Fig. 12. Throughput versus payload size

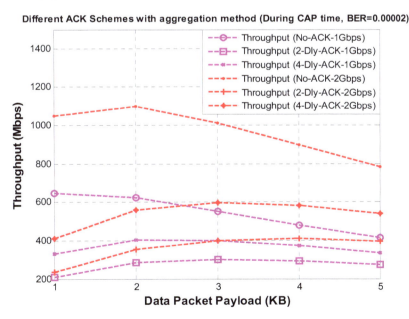

Fig. 13. Throughput versus payload size

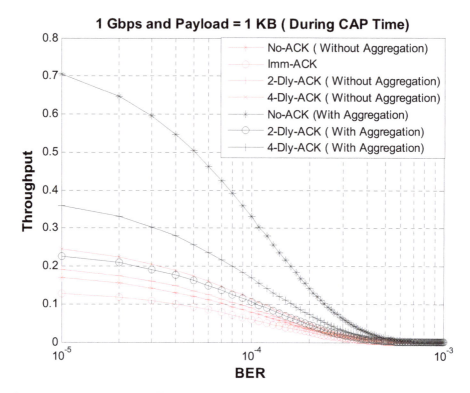

Fig. 14. Throughput versus BER value with different ACK policies

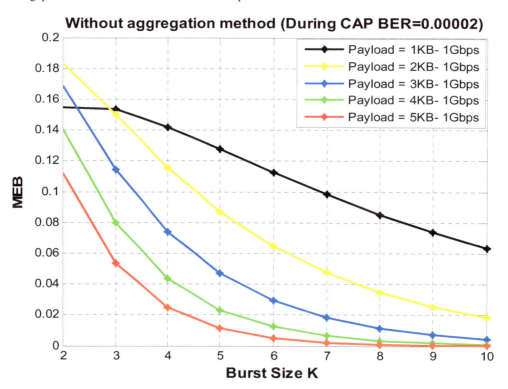

Fig. 15. MEB versus burst size

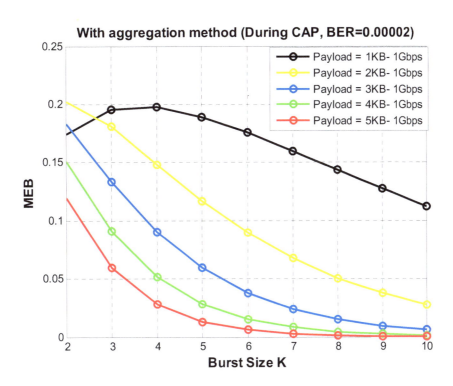

Fig. 16. MEB versus burst size

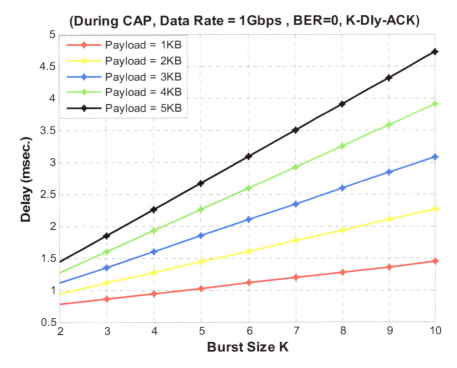

Fig. 17. Access delay versus burst size

FUTURE RESEARCH DIRECTIONS

The majority of the discussion so far has focused on the overview and MAC designing of UWB system as it is today. In this section, however, we outline some future application scenarios which may shape future evaluation of this system [19].

Integral part of 4G communications networks: The new communication era is going to be 4G, where personal area network, local/home area networks, cellular and wider area communication all will integrate with each other. Thus, with the application of UWB technology it is possible to reach 4G.

3D Imaging technology: 3D technology is the emerging technology in the field of visual communication and display technology. The wireless interconnection of such technologies would naturally require a higher data rate compared to conventional image transmissions. With UWB applications including the provision of image transmission, it should consider the requirements for supporting 3D image transmissions.

Digital implementation solutions: Currently, AD/DA conversion technology is not sufficient to support all the requirements of UWB technology, once it is achieve, a door to UWB technology would be opened for digital implementation and signal processing techniques.

Super-high density networks: The future UWB systems will require suitable spectrum recourses management schemes in order to support the demand for high data rates to an increased number of network nodes. Typical examples include UWB wireless sensor networks and UWB Ad-hoc networks with large number of nodes.

Aforementioned applications of UWB systems are foreseen to be the main stream research efforts in the future. However, there are several issues to be addresses both at physical and MAC layers for proper implementation of UWB systems [7]. These issues are as follow:

∞With existing technology, it is very hard to avoid the pulse distortion caused by antennas and dispersive-propagation environment. As of now pulse based system don't have a front-end filter to completely remove the pulse distortion hence, it's very difficult to tune the UWB transceivers for high data rate applications.

∞The current receiver structures need more research and evaluation, especially for timing acquisition issue in system. A RAKE structure is suggested in many research papers but the channel estimation and synchronization required for RAKE are too difficult for short UWB pulses. So we need some other alternative or suboptimum solutions for the same.

∞A small change in tuning of accuracy, ranging and detection capabilities of UWB can effect a lot to network design .Thus, it is important to pay a good attention on the cross-layer design between the physical layer and MAC layer of a UWB system.

∞For any military or commercial application a secure communication is must. Lots of research efforts are still needed to enhance the security of UWB system; especially the   rich multipath in the UWB channel can be exploited. A time reversals technique can be a good candidate for the same.

∞A proper infrastructure is needed to validate the above system and network concepts. The lack of test bed or such experimental facility is choking the progress of R&D in UWB system.

SUMMARY

In this chapter we presented the state of the art of UWB wireless technology and highlighted key application areas, technological challenges, and future research directions. As UWB is a potential technology in next generation communication, we need to design better MAC protocols, routing and related networks protocols. Here, we presented a performance analysis of UWB WPAN (IEEE 802.15.3) MAC for wireless sensor networks and showed the impact of various acknowledgment schemes on multiple access capacity under different parameters. The optimal payload size as well as optimal burst size can be determined analytically from the presented analysis. On concluding note, we hope this chapter will provide basic concepts of UWB MAC standard and will also serve as an initial starting point for students, researcher, and engineer in the filed of wireless sensor networks.

REFERENCES

[1]   FCC, Revision of Part 15 of the Commission's Rules Regarding Ultra- Wideband Transmission Systems. First Report and Order, ET Docket 98-153, February, 2002.

[2]   WUSB Alliance, Wireless USB, from http://www.usb.org/wusb/home

[3]   Staccato Communications Inc. " Wireless USB: the Time is Now", from http://www.staccatocommunications.com/products/

[4]   P802.15.3/D17. (C/LM) Standard for Telecommunications and Information Exchange Between Systems (2003). LAN/MAN Specific Requirements-Part 15.3: Wireless Medium Access Control (MAC) and Physical Layer (PHY) Specifications for High Rate Wireless Personal Area Networks. February, 2003.

[5]   R. Fisher, R. Kohno, M. M. Laughlin & M. Welborn, ".DS-UWB Physical Layer," *Submission to 802.15 Task Group 3a*, IEEE 802.15-04/0137r4, January, 2005.

[6]   A.Batra, "Multi-band OFDM Physical Layer," *Proposal for IEEE 802.15 Task Group 3a,* IEEE 802.15-04/0493r1, September, 2004.

[7]   X. Shen, M. Guizani, R. Caiming, & T. L. Hgo (Ed.), *"Ultra-Wideband Wireless Communications and Network,"* John Wiley & Sons. 2006

[8]   IEEE 802.15 WPAN High Rate Alternative PHY Task Group 3a (TG3a) (2005), from http://www.ieee802.org/15/pub/TG3a.html

[9]   Y. Xaio, X. Shen, and H. Jiang, "Optimal ACK Mechanisum of the IEEE 802.15.3 MAC for Ultra-Wideband Systems," IEEE JSAC, Vol.24, No.4, April, 2006.

[10]   H. Chen, Z. Guo, R. Yao, and Y. Li, "Improved Performance with Adaptive Dly-ACK for IEEE 802.15.3 WPAN over UWB PHY", IEICE TRANS. Fundamentals, VOl-E88-A, No.9, Sep. 2005.

[11]   Y. Xaio, " IEEE 802.11n:Enhancements for higher throughput in wireless LANs," IEEE Communications, December 2005. pp.82-91.

[12]   S.Mehta et.al, " Performance Issue in terms of ACK policies with/without Aggregation", IEEE P802.15 Working Group for Wireless Personal Area Networks (WPANs),,DOC: IEEE 802.15-08-0124-00-003c, March 2008.

[13]   K.-W. Chin and D. Lowe, "Simulation study of the IEEE 802.15.3 MAC," in: Proc., Australian Telecommunications and Network Applications Conference (ATNAC), Sydney, Australia, 2004.

[14]   Y. H. Tseng, E. H. Wu, and G. H. Chen., "Maximum Traffic Scheduling and Capacity Analysis for IEEE 802.15.3 High Data Rate MAC Protocol," in proc. of IEEE VTC, 2003.

[15]   G. Bianchi, " Performance analysis of the IEEE 802.11 distributed coordination function," IEEE JSAC, Vol.18, no-3, pp.535-547, Mar.2000.

[16]   Y. Xiao, and J. Rosdahl, " Throughput and Delay Limits of IEEE 802.11," IEEE Communication Letters, Vol.6, No.8, August 2002

[17]   H.Chen, Z. Guo, R. Y. Yao, X. Shen, and Y.Li ," Perfoamnce Analyis of delyed Acknowledgemnet Scheme in UWB-Based High-Rate WPAN," IEEE transaction on vehicular technology, Vol.55, No.2, March 2006.

[18]   H. Harada et. al., " IEEE P802.15 Working Group for Wireless Personal Area Networks (WPANs)", IEEE P802.15 Working Group for Wireless Personal Area Networks (WPANs) DOC: IEEE 802.15-07-0761-05-003c, July 2007.

[19]   B. Allen et. al, "Ultra Wideband: Technology and Future perspective," , White paper, King's College, London.,2005.

## CHAPTER 6

Smart Agriculture

Aqeel-ur-Rehman and Zubair A. Shaikh

*Center for Research in Ubiquitous Computing (CRUC), Department of Computer Science,
National University of Computer and Emerging Sciences (FAST-NU), Karachi, Pakistan.*

Abstract: Use of technology in different areas to get numerous benefits is itself a valuable research. Use of Sensor network in the area of agriculture is not new. But due to the different weather, soil, water and land conditions, diverse models, methods of analysis and solutions are needed on which different communities of researchers are working and proposing several solutions. That instigates need of some different ways specifically for agriculture that can be helpful in developing solution for different conditions.

Ubiquitous Computing and Context-Aware Computing are highlighting the approaches to deal with variability in conditions, situations and problems. The combination of different technologies and their application towards certain area is always been a challenging task. The combination of emerging technologies including ubiquitous computing, context-aware computing and grid computing with sensor network can be applied on agriculture domain to make the agriculture smarter.

In this chapter, the concept of Smart Agriculture is described and use of different advanced technologies towards the agriculture domain is highlighted. The evolution of agriculture through the support of different advanced technologies is also presented. Some details about the development of smart agriculture prototype for irrigation control are also the part of this chapter.

INTRODUCTION

Different areas of life are getting a great impact by the advancements in technology. From many years, people are working towards the automation with some level of intelligence to replace or minimize the human factor from the processes. The current trends envisaging that the next era will be moving around the concept of Ubiquitous Computing [1] and Context-Aware Computing [2].

It is an observation that the word "Smart" is appearing as a buzz word with many areas of life like Smart Office [3], Smart University [4], Smart Hospital [5], Smart Farm [6] *etc.* There is a need of understanding first that what does the word *Smart* mean? The Webster dictionary meaning of "*Smart*" as adjective is clever, knowledgeable, and intelligent *etc.* This exemplify that researchers are working towards developing the autonomous systems that could take some level of decisions by their own in different levels of complex circumstances.

Researchers are contributing towards smart agriculture by developing different project related to land and plant monitoring, precision irrigation, precision farming, crop disease monitoring, cattle farming, animal behavior monitoring and pastures assessment *etc.* Sensor networks are playing a vital role in measuring the in-field variability to support on-time decision making.

In this chapter, authors' opinion towards Smart Agriculture is presented.

DEFINING SMART AGRICULTURE

Smart Agriculture could be defined as "*an approach to understand the basic requirements as well as the changes in current environment due to external factors based on the context information and utilization of collected data to optimize sensors' operation or influence the operations of actuators to change the current environment"*.

Smart Agriculture is based on the following steps:

1. Sensing local agricultural parameters
2. Identification of sensing location and data gathering
3. Transferring data from crop field to control station for decision making
4. Decision making based on local data, domain knowledge and history
5. Actuation and Control based on decision

It is obvious that the optimization of sensors' operations will be towards the better development of the crop or plant.

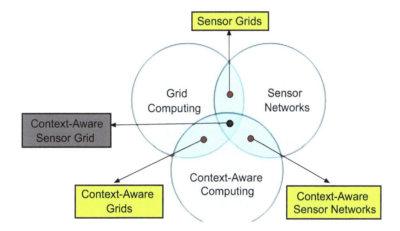

Fig. 1. Technology Integration

The concept of smart agriculture is based on integration of three well known technologies that are Sensor Network technology, Grid Computing technology and Context-aware Computing technology.

The first three steps and the last step of smart agriculture process are supported by the sensor network technology as it requires sensing and communication. Satellite navigation technology is also used to support the sensor network collected data to acquire the location of sensors as well as actuators. This location related data plays an important role in decision making to know the exact area under effect. Grid computing technology supports in providing the low cost high power computing and distributed data storage facility. Both the above mentioned facilities are of extreme need as sensor network generates huge amount of sensed data that requires heavy amount of storage space as well as the high computing power for processing and decision making procedures. The use of grid computing also supports the cause of low cost solution development. Fourth step of the process involves grid computing facility and the context-aware computing facility. Context-aware computing is an aid to model the exact situation based on the sensed data. Context-awareness supports the decision making process to formulate the aroused problem and its solution based on the current and history data considering their relationship with the problem. In other words, context-aware computing offers generalization to the procedure to deal with variety of problems.

APPLICATION OF TECHNOLOGIES IN AGRICULTURE

Advancements and innovations of different technologies also benefited the agriculture domain. Among many technologies, Satellite navigation technology and the sensor network technology are the first two technologies that are actively in use for monitoring and data collection of the said domain area. The other technologies that are becoming the part of the said domain are grid computing technology, ubiquitous computing technology and the context-aware computing technology. Following are the brief introduction of the above mentioned technologies:

Satellite Navigation Technology

NAVSTAR Global Positioning System (NAVSTAR GPS) became available for civilian use in 1996 [7]. Since then it is utilized to find vehicle location and navigation as well as the sensor and actuator position. GPS technology providing the benefit to get the location based agriculture land and crop monitoring. That makes easier to take decisions on the basis of local data instead of global data values. This technology is also helpful for autopilot operations of tractors and other machinery.

Sensor Network Technology

Sensors and their networks are in use in agriculture [8] for crop monitoring, local weather monitoring, soil attributes monitoring *etc.* All the data gathered through sensors is used for either analysis purpose or for decision making to switch actuators.

Sensor are used mostly to measure air temperature, humidity, ambient light, soil temperature, soil moisture, soil pH value, air speed, air direction *etc.*

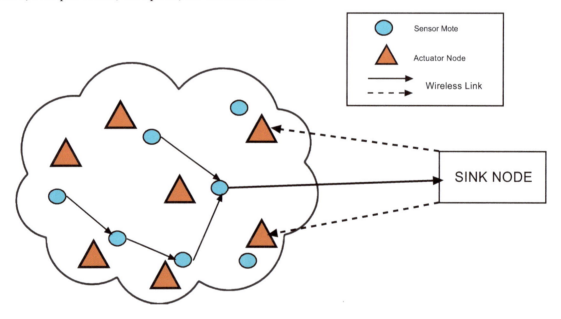

Fig. 2. Semi-Automated Wireless Sensor and Actuator Network (WSAN)

Grid Computing Technology

Grid computing [9] concept is to share the heterogeneous devices and components over a large distributed geographical area. The use of this technology in the domain of agriculture is gradually started to increase due to the utilization of sensor network technology. Grid technology is providing the shared data storage and high computational power to store and process the huge sensed data.

Ubiquitous Computing Technology

Ubiquitous computing technology presents computing everywhere concept by providing seamless integration of the devices to work autonomously based on the predefined settings as well as the current changes in the situation. Use of this technology is providing the in-field computation power with the help of WSAN to deal with variety of agriculture related problems.

Context-Aware Computing Technology

Context-awareness is an important part of ubiquitous or pervasive computing. A system is context-aware if it can extract, interpret and react to the context information and adjust its functionality to the current context. Context is defined by Anind K. Dey *et al.* [10] as:

"Context is any information that can be used to characterize the situation of an entity. An entity is a person, place, or object that is considered relevant to the interaction between a user and an application, including the user and application themselves".

Due to the different weather, soil, water and land conditions, diverse models, methods of analysis and solutions are needed in agriculture. Context-aware computing technology is highlighting the approach to deal with variability in conditions, situations and problems. Use of the said technology is already started to deal with agriculture related problems [11, 12, 13].

PROBLEMS RELATED TO AGRICULTURE

There are many different problems in this area. Some major problems that instigate the use of technology are described below:

Irrigation

Irrigation is one of the most important areas of agriculture. It is defined as the artificial application of water. It is helpful in those areas where rainfalls are not enough to fulfill the crop water requirements. Water shortage is becoming the global problem. This instigates the need of proper use of water that is water should be provided to only those places where it is needed and in required quantity. In addition of that water wastage is also desired to be minimized. To cope up with these requirements many different methods of irrigation are in use like drip irrigation, sprinkler irrigation *etc.* The purpose of different methods of irrigation is controlled water distribution at the required places so that the water could be saved without compromising the crop water requirements. To find out amount of water required at specific location on a particular instance of time, Information Technology (IT) is playing a vital role in providing different solutions.

Pesticide and Fertilizer Application

Use of fertilizers and pesticides at a proper location and quantity increases the productivity of the yield. Application of fertilizers could be performed using several methods including broadcasting, placement and foliar application. Selection of application method is based on the crop as well as the method of cultivation. Distribution of required quantity of fertilizer at proper place is a challenging task. Applying unnecessary amount of fertilizers may deteriorate the quality of water as well as could support the growth of algae.

Pesticide application is a treatment of organism (e.g. crop) from possible damages by other plants, fungus, insects or animals. Timing, quantity and location of application are very critical in case of pesticides spraying.

Use of technologies is becoming a great support in dealing with timing, quantity control, and finding proper location in demand for pesticides and fertilizers.

Crop, Soil and Climate Monitoring

Monitoring is an important aspect of agriculture. Knowing the state of crop, soil and climate is crucial for farmers as their decisions to irrigate crop, spray pesticide, apply fertilizer *etc.* are based on their states. Physical monitoring for a large agriculture land does not produce good results as it is almost impossible to perform monitoring 24 hours as well as to keep on check for multiple variants at a time.

Sensor network technology is successfully in use to get the local micro climate measurement as well as to measure soil attributes and the plant state [14]. The combination of technologies is also providing the benefit to have a mix of several local and global attributes to attain a good decision.

Cattle Farming

Cattle farming also come under the agriculture domain. Live stock production [15] is not only contributing towards meat production and cultivate animal products (like wool, leather, milk *etc.*) but also helpful for work (like cultivate fields, harvest crops *etc.*). Many of the animals feed source is grassland. Knowing the state of the grassland pastures is very important for the farmers. As farmers have to decide for pastures irrigation, application of fertilizers or to move animals to other green pasture. To make the decisions optimal, advanced computer and network technology could be helpful in this regard [6].

FROM PAST TO PRESENT

Agriculture is one of the most important areas on which human life is very much dependent. In the era before industrialization, vast majority of human population was engaged in the sector of agriculture. By using different techniques, people kept on trying to increase the productivity. The use of mechanization in the form of Tractor was started in late 19th century to speedup the farming tasks to such a level that was impossible manually.

Due to the increase in human population, the demand of food also increases that leads the use of different technologies in agriculture. Sensors were the first among advanced technologies that were used to get soil attributes specially the soil moisture. The use of sensor technology was started in late 1980s [8, 16, 17]. Availability of GPS technology in support of the sensor network technology provided the basis for Precision Agriculture (PA). To get enhanced productivity while conserving water, Precision Agriculture became one of the tools that drew world's attention in early 1990s.

PA is defined and termed in many ways like Variable Rate Technology (VRT), Precision Farming, Global Positioning System (GPS) Agriculture, Farming by Inch, Information-Intensive Agriculture, Site Specific Crop Management *etc.* [18] but the underlying concept remains the same. PA is an agriculture concept based on the in-field variability. It is considered as the application of information technology in addition with the experiences to get optimized production efficiency with optimized quality having the minimized risk and the environmental impacts [14].

The agricultural-research community is working on different aspects of agriculture to improve the quality of farming as well as the productivity of agriculture land. The community has undertaken numerous pilot projects. Some of the projects are discussed below:

Many different projects were developed for the scouting of crops and the different weather and soil attributes of agriculture land [8, 17, 19]. Carnegie Mellon University researchers developed a small wireless sensor network to monitor plant nursery [20]. Sensors were deployed to measure air temperature, relative humidity, soil moisture, soil temperature and light. A GUI based application provided support to view and analyze the collected information. Sensor networks also been used to overcome fungus and pests problems. Aline Baggio at Delft University of Technology [21] developed a project to deal the potato crop disease. Sensors were used to sense humidity and temperature. Monitoring of these two facts helped them to reduce the disease. Cattle farming that also very much dependent on agriculture domain, has some other issues like animal welfare, food safety and environmental effects *etc.* Tim Wark and his other team members [6] at CSIRO ICT center, Australia created a pervasive, self configurable sensor based solution to analyze the behavior of animals (sleeping, grazing, ruminating *etc.*) and their control as well as the pastures assessment.

Emergence of Wireless Sensor and Actuator Networks (WSAN) in this decade provided a platform to go further from monitoring to the control. Irrigation control is one of the important areas in agriculture. Several sensor based projects have been developed [22, 23] specifically for controlling irrigation water keeping its importance for increasing yields. Tapankumar *et al.* [22] designed and developed a computer based drip irrigation control system having the facility of remote data acquisition. They also presented the benefits of storing sensors data for statistical analysis to find out the irrigation requirements for different crops. While Yunseop Kim *et al.* [23] developed an electronically controlled sensor based irrigation system that provides the facility to monitor soil moisture and temperature, weather information and sprinkler position remotely using the Bluetooth and GPS technologies. The concept behind the development of their project was to maximize productivity while saving water.

Grid Computing and Context-Aware Computing are also in the line of other advanced technologies that are providing benefits to the agriculture domain. These technologies are the part of different research projects [11, 12, 13] that made easy to deal with variety of problems in different weather and soil conditions. The PLANTS project [11] is based on the idea of providing seamless communication between plants and other artifacts for different scenarios ranging from domestic plant to precision agriculture. During the research phase of the project, Christos Goumopoulos *et al.* introduced the term 'Proactive Agriculture' emphasizing that the proactive computing approach is highly beneficial for agriculture domain. To provide the

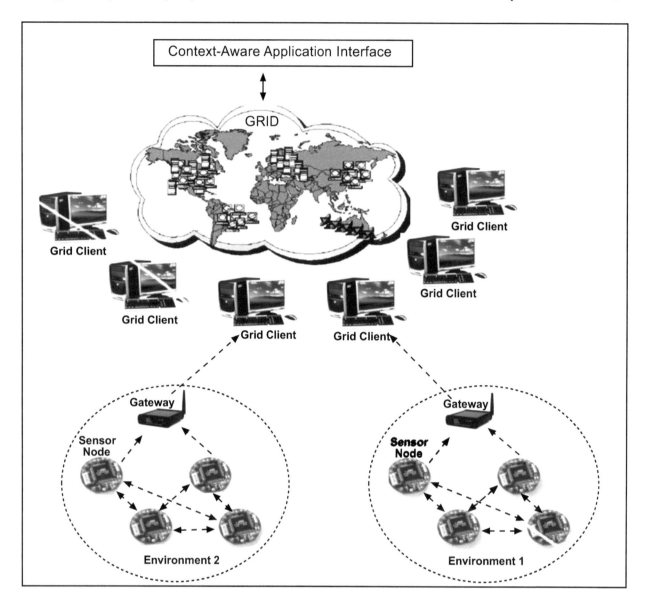

Fig. 3. Context-Aware Sensor Grid Architecture [12].

advantages of the said technologies, we presented a context-aware sensor grid framework for agriculture [12] (see figure 4) that emphasis the use of grid computing technology to have benefit of shared distributed storage as well as the world-wide access of deployed WSAN system. The same idea of using grid technology to benefit agriculture domain is in implementation phase in Malaysia as a part of the project namely "KnowledgeGRID Malaysia".

PROTOTYPE DEVELOPMENT

A prototype was developed to have proof of concept for smart agriculture. The prototype was based on Context-Aware Sensor Grid Framework [12]. The hardware of system comprised on:

o TelosB sensor motes
o Ech2o-20 soil moisture probes
o Desktop PCs

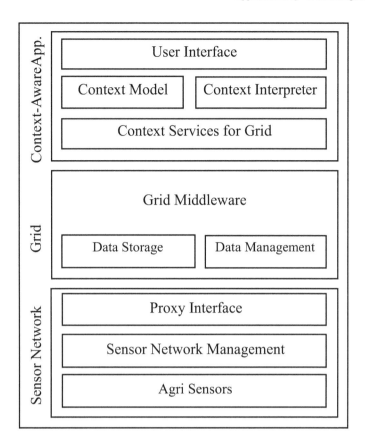

Fig. 4. Context-Aware Sensor Grid Framework for Agriculture [12].

Six sensor motes were used to cover two zones having three motes each. Every mote has built-in temperature, ambient light and air humidity sensors. Ech2o-20 soil moisture probe was attached to get soil moisture contents with each mote. One mote was used as sink mote to collect the sensor network data. The sink mote was attached via serial interface with the base station desktop PC. Every zone has an actuator mote connected with sprinkler. It is controlled via ZigBee communication module through base station node. The base station PC was placed as a node to the desktop grid computing environment that was having some dedicated and non-dedicated desktop systems to get large shared distributed storage and high computing power.

The application was developed using C# on .Net Platform. To achieve context-awareness ontology based modeling was used to model current context. "Jena" with SWRL (Semantic Web Rule Language) rule engine and SQWRL (Semantic Query-Enhanced Web Rule Language) query language were utilized for OWL ontology reasoning. The whole setup was to model the crop irrigation problem for variety of crops. The ontology was developed using Protégé that provided the relationships between crops, soil, local atmosphere and the system components.

Alchemi desktop grid toolkit was used to develop the grid computing environment. Database facility was achieved using SQL server. In SQL databases, the aggregated sampled data was stored that facilitates the decision support system in finding the exact current situation.

The wireless sensor and actuator network was built using TinyOS programming facility. The semi-automated WSAN setup was used (see figure 2). The sensors were setup to send samples on after every 5 minutes. The collected data was then aggregated and utilized by decision support system after every 15 minutes to model the current context using the ontology. In case of any stress conditions like temperature stress, irrigation stress etc. decision is formalized and forwarded to the attached devices for necessary action. The decision could be an alarming text message for a mobile phone or an e-mail message or an actuation string to actuate the concerned sprinkler.

The prototype implementation was a success as it detected correctly the different stress conditions and initiated the remedies described. The specified remedies were the actuation of sprinklers for misting or for irrigation, generating the alarming messages and send it to specified mobile phones or send the message through e-mail. The developed prototype was able to deal with the irrigation problem. The prototype can be extended to cope with multiple problems like pesticide spraying, fertilization etc. The major change that will be needed is the extension in the ontology for different desirable problem solutions.

THE FUTURE

Utilization of advanced technologies and networks is taking us towards the smarter world. Smart agriculture concept is to go from specialization to the generalization of solutions for the problems. The agriculture domain requires low cost, easy to deploy and use solutions. This could only be possible if we start to think globally instead of locally. On the large scale, solutions that could deal with variety of challenges of different domains will become cheaper than the specialized solutions. In this regard, utility on demand and service oriented concepts realization is of great demand. Grid computing is one of the approaches that could support the concept of smart agriculture but the complexities in realization of grid computing environment puts a hurdle on its path. The newly developed concept of Cloud Computing is presenting itself a good candidate for the future of smart agriculture through which the specialized and dedicated hardware for storage and computing will not be required to install on site. That will reduce the hassle of administration, installation and the cost as well.

CONCLUSION

In this chapter, the authors presented the concept of smart agriculture. Increase in population and demand for food requires some new methods that could increase the production multiple times utilizing the even lesser resources as shortage of water is increasing day by day and agriculture land is also decreasing. Use of advanced technologies could help us in this regard. The concept of smart agriculture presented could be helpful in achieving the above mentioned goal. Smart agriculture concept is the utilization of different advanced technologies together with the experiences of people as well as the results of the historic events to engender better solution of the problems.

The technologies that were highlighted in this chapter are sensor network technology, satellite navigation technology, grid computing technology, ubiquitous computing technology, context aware computing technology and the cloud computing technology.

ACKNOWLEDGEMENT

The work in this article is in part supported by Higher Education Commission, Pakistan and Centre for Research in Ubiquitous Computing (CRUC) at National University of Computer and Emerging Sciences (FAST-NU), Karachi, Pakistan.

REFERENCES

[1]   Mark Weiser, "The computer of the 21st century", Scientific American, vol 265(3), pp.66-75, September 1991.

[2]   B. Schilit, N. Adams, and R. Want, "Context-aware computing applications", in IEEE Workshop on Mobile Computing Systems and Applications (WMCSA'94), Santa Cruz, CA, US, 1994, pp. 89-101.

[3]   A. Ahmed, A. S. Quraishi, Z. Sattar and Z. B. Alam, ""RFID based smart office", B.S. thesis, Department of Electrical Engineering, National University of Computer and Emerging Sciences, Karachi, Pakistan, 2008.

[4]   Aqeel-ur-Rehman, Abu Zafar Abbasi and Zubair A. Shaikh, "Building a smart university using RFID technology", in International Conference on Computer Science and Software Engineering, 2008 Volume 5, 2008, pp. 641 – 644.

[5]   P. Fuhrer and D. Guinard, "Building a smart hospital using RFID technologies", in 1st European Conference on eHealth Fribourg, Switzerland, 12-13 October 2006, Fribourg, Switzerland, 2006, pp. 1-14.

[6]   Tim Wark, Peter Corke, Pavan Sikka *et al.* "Transforming agriculture through pervasive Wireless Sensor Networks," IEEE Pervasive Computing, vol. 6, no. 2, pp. 50-57, Apr.-June 2007.

[7]   National Archives and Records Administration, U.S. Global Positioning System Policy. March 29, 1996. [Online] Available: http://clinton4.nara.gov/textonly/WH/EOP/OSTP/html/gps-factsheet.html . [Accessed August 04, 2009]

[8]   N. Wang, NQ Zhang and MH Wang, "Wireless sensors in agriculture and food industry - Recent development and future perspective", in Computers and Electronics in Agriculture Journal, Vol.50 (1), pp. 1-14, 2006.

[9]   I. Foster and C. Kesselman, The Grid: Blueprint for a New Computing Infrastructure. Morgan Kaufmann Publishers, 1st Edition 1999, 2nd Edition 2003.

[10]   Anind K. Dey, Daniel Salber and Gregory D. Abowd, "A conceptual framework and a toolkit for supporting the rapid prototyping of context-Aware applications", Anchor article of a special issue on context-aware computing in the Human-Computer Interaction (HCI) Journal, Volume 16 (2-4), pp. 97-166, 2001.

[11]   C. Goumopoulos, A. Kameas, and B. O Flynn, "Proactive agriculture: an integrated framework for developing distributed hybrid systems," Lecture Notes in Computer Science, vol. 4611, pp. 214, 2007.

[12]   Aqeel-ur-Rehman and Zubair A. Shaikh, "Towards design of context-aware sensor grid framework for agriculture", in Fifth International Conference on Information Technology (ICIT 2008), XXVIII-WASET Conference, Rome, Italy, 2008, pp. 244-247.

[13]   C. Goumopoulos, A. Kameas and A. Cassells, "An Ontology-driven system architecture for precision agriculture applications", in International Journal of Metadata, Semantics and Ontologies (IJMSO), pp. 72-84, 2009.

[14]   James Taylor and Brett Whelan, "A General Introduction to Precision Agriculture", Australian Center for Precision Agriculture, 2005. [Online]   Available: www.usyd.edu.au/su/agric/acpa. [Accessed August 04, 2009].

[15]   C. Sere, H. Steinfeld and J. Groeneweld, "Description of systems in world livestock systems - Current status issues and trends", U.N. Food and Agriculture Organization, Rome, Italy, 1995. [Accessed on August 04, 2009].

[16]   Adamchuk VI, Hummel JW, Morgan MT and Upadhyaya SK, "On-the-go soil sensors for precision agriculture", Computers and Electronics in Agriculture, vol. 44, pp. 71-91, 2004.

[17]   A. Hemmat and V. I. Adamchuk, "Sensor systems for measuring soil compaction: Review and analysis", Computers and Electronics in Agriculture, vol. 63(2), pp. 89-103, 2008.

[18]   Ancha Srinivasan, Ed., Handbook of Precision Agriculture: Principles and Applications. 2006.

[19]   Camilli, A., C. E. Cugnasca, A. M. Saraiva, A. R. Hirakawa, and P. L. P. Correa, "From wireless sensors to field mapping: Anatomy of an application for precision agriculture", Computers and Electronics in Agriculture, vol. 58, pp. 25–36, 2007.

[20]   W. Zhang, G. Kantor, and S. Singh, "Integrated Wireless Sensor/Actuator Networks in an Agricultural Application," in 2nd ACM Int'l Conf. Embedded Networked Sensor Systems (SENSYS 04), ACM Press, 2004, pp. 317.

[21]   A. Baggio, "Wireless Sensor Networks in Precision Agriculture," in ACM Workshop Real-World Wireless Sensor Networks, 2005.

[22]   Tapankumar Basu, Vijaya R. Thool, Ravindra C. Thool and Anjali C. Birajdar, "Computer based drip irrigation control system with remote data acquisition system", in 4th World Congress of Computers in Agriculture and Natural Resources, USA, July 2006.

[23]   Y. Kim, R.G. Evans, and W. Iversen, "Remote sensing and control of irrigation system using a distributed wireless sensor network", IEEE Transactions on Instrumentation and Measurement, Volume 57, Issue 7, pp. 1379 – 1387, 2008.

AUTHOR INDEX

SUBJECT INDEX

www.ingramcontent.com/pod-product-compliance
Lightning Source LLC
Chambersburg PA
CBHW041418050326
40689CB00002B/560